She's Not Exotic Like Iranian Girls.

She's Not Exotic Like Iranian Girls.

Sima Nahan

URTEXT*media*

Cover design by Laila Parsi

ISBN: 978-0-9994437-0-5

Published by URTEXT*media*
www.urtext.us

Printed in the United States of America

Contents

King of the World   7

Good Luck in Ghana   24

Since There Is No Help   30

Love of a Good Man   39

She's Not Exotic Like Iranian Girls   64

Two Thousand Five Hundred Years   76

Exotica   87
    The Color Black
    Black Blood (what have you done)
    The Party
    The Black Hole of Survival
    Digital Reconstruction
    What have you done, cont.
    The End

Country Pop   113

KING OF THE WORLD

The kids and the gear were piled in the back of the Land Rover. Roya's father and uncle were in the front, sometimes one and sometimes the other behind the wheel. The ride was pretty rough but the kids didn't mind. They were bouncy teenagers who burst out laughing when the bumps or sudden swerves ejected their bottoms from the pull-down seats. There were no seatbelts back then but the kids knew no danger. They felt nothing if not safe.

Before everybody suddenly left there were a lot of kids in the back of the Land Rover: Roya, her brother, a couple of his friends, and her best friend Katayoun. The boys had their own interests and the girls their own but they all lived for Fridays. School ran Monday through Wednesday full days, and half-day on Thursdays. Thursday afternoons were spent in excited anticipation of the Friday ski trips. Dads were in charge of the preparations, from the chains to the equipment to the lunch, and moms had Fridays to themselves, at home.

The fifty-mile drive to Dizin was an adventure in itself. They set out early in the morning and stopped in

Karaj to pick up freshly baked sandwich bread before the trucks arrived for distribution in Tehran. The kids went through a few loaves for breakfast, munching while wiping the windows that were steamed up from the load of hot bread. Road conditions were often treacherous but unless an avalanche had completely blocked the road the Land Rover managed to push though, often in first gear. The kids waved triumphantly when they passed cars that had to turn back. Even four-wheel drives required chains.

Turning off the main road that wound up and down the mountains toward the Caspian Sea, the road to Dizin passed through the village of Velat Rood (Velayat Rood, to be precise). This little village supplied the ski resort with most of its labor force and some of its best skiers. Occasionally, if there was a long weekend, Roya and family stayed overnight in the village. They slept in unheated cottages where they dined, in full ski attire, on rice steamed with wild herbs and fried eggs. In the mornings the river was frozen over so they had to break the ice to brush their teeth. The whole experience was cold and uncomfortable but deeply gratifying.

Around the bend a few miles down the road from Velat Rood, the big Hotel Dizin and a number of posh chalets came into view. Pulling on stiff, icy ski boots that had spent the night in the back of the Land Rover was not very pleasant. They all groaned as they forced their feet clad in thick socks into the unyielding boots. Carrying their skis to the gondola they stamped their feet to get the blood flowing. But once they stepped off the asphalt of the parking lot onto the snow, all cold and discomfort was forgotten. The fresh snow squeaking underfoot made Roya's heart sing. Another glorious day on the slopes! At nine-thousand feet at the base, the spectacular mountain expanse with some of the best snow on the planet, was worth any hardship.

"I don't like this guy," Roya whispered to her father one morning as they waited in the gondola line. She discretely motioned toward a short middle-aged guy in expensive attire and gleaming gear. Her dad raised his eyebrows: "You know who this is?" She didn't. He nodded that he will tell her later. Later he said that the guy was reputed to be the richest man in Iran, rich from kickbacks on arms deals. There was a peculiar smile that Roya's dad gave her on occasions such as this.

Dizin, or Gajereh as it was known to old-timers, was a microcosm of sorts. There were distinct groups that went skiing, each keeping to its own kind. The biggest group were the *taqootis*. This was a moniker that appeared after the revolution referring to a certain stone idol named Taqoot that Muhammad had crushed to smithereens in Mecca. The taqootis of the French revolution were called the *ancien régime*. The little rich man that Roya had noticed was among the top tier of this group, though he fled to the U.S. with his money before he lost his head.

The second group, in stark contrast to the first, were the locals who were also the best skiers. These were young men from the village who skied seriously and had Olympics ambitions. They gave lessons, operated the lifts, drove the snow-packing machines, maintained the slopes in summertime, and had permanently tanned faces and arms. They treated the taqootis with deference, though their superior skiing elevated them in everybody's eyes. Roya knew a few of these guys by name but that was all. She was on friendly terms with one boy from the village, a tall boy a few years younger than herself named

Mokhtar, who liked to follow her on the slopes calling out Roya, Roya, Roya, his big white teeth gleaming in his dark sun-burnt face. But probably because he did not enjoy the kind of leisure that Roya and her friends did, he was not always found on the slopes.

Another group was comprised of unlikely skiers. These were university students with Stalinesque mustaches and permanent scowls on their face. They were the leftists, the commies, the enemy of the taqootis. Their sour expression was to remind everyone that they did not approve of Dizin or skiing but had to be there out of duty. Their "duty" was to train for God knows what guerilla activity they had in mind. In the summers they were vigorous mountaineers and in winter, having no other sporting outlet, they were resigned to skiing to stay in shape. In the summer they hiked carrying stones in their backpacks to toughen their characters and strengthen their frames. They slept and ate with villagers in remote areas to "proletarize" themselves. Young as Roya was, and intimidating as these guys acted, she found them a little ridiculous. The proletariat wanted to train for the Olympics but it looked liked these guys had other plans for them.

Then there were the foreigners. Some of these were families who were stationed in Iran for business or political reasons and kept to themselves on and off the slopes. But there were also solo foreigners, most of them young men. There were the occasional American "hot dog" skiers in blue jeans soaked to the knees and icicles dangling from sweaters poking from under their parkas. They wowed everyone with their shenanigans. There were young European males who appeared to be under strict instruction not to mingle with the natives, especially of the female variety. They slalomed nicely. And then of course there was Jean-Claude, the good-looking curly-haired French dandy who broke all the rules. He appeared not to be up to much other than ski on weekends and bed good-looking Iranian women the rest of the time. His escapades were the talk of the slopes.

Roya of course skied with her own set, which was composed of her family and their close friends. To outsiders they might have appeared taqooti but that's not what they thought of themselves. They belonged more to the intelligentsia of Iran. They were literary types, intellectuals, and worked mostly in publishing or were technocrats of some sort. They were critical, confident, and cool. They liked the best of all possible worlds. One of Roya's dad's friends wore a cowboy hat with a bandana tucked underneath to cover his neck *kafiyeh* style. Tearing down the mountains with the scarf flapping in the wind he was called the flying Arab cowboy.

Roya and Katti dodged their fathers and brothers as soon as they got off the four-person gondola and dashed to the two-seater chair lifts. Nobody usually saw them until the end of the day when they could be found begging the chair lift attendants for one last run before shutting down for the day. They rarely gave up before Katti's father who was the stricter one let out his angry *Ka-Ta-Youn* at the top of his voice to get them to turn around and head downhill. On the chairlift the girls went wild. They sang from the minute they pulled down the safety bar until they hopped off and glided to a stop. They belted out lyrics that they barely understood: The Beatles, Cat Stevens, Creedence Clearwater Revival... They tried singing harmony like Simon and Garfunkel but neither being very talented they only made themselves laugh hysterically. They yelled out "California dreamin' on such a winter's day" while spreading their arms to embrace the glistening winter's day around them. Once they screeched "light my fire, light my fire, light my fire" for the entire ride and were hoarse for the rest of the day. Occasionally someone skiing down below looked up at them curiously and the girls energetically waved and hollered exaggerated greetings to them.

At lunch time they stopped by the veranda of the lodge, unbuckled their boots, fumbled in their backpacks with numbed fingers, and fished out the *halvardeh* sandwiches that they had made that morning in the back of the Land Rover. The butter in the sandwiches was by this time so cold it stuck to the roof of their mouths. The taqootis ate hot lunches by the fireplace in the lodge; they were lightweights. Roya rarely went inside the building except to use the bathroom. Once, as she flung open the door to go inside, she slammed into His Majesty. They were both startled. As the Shah stabilized Roya wobbling in her heavy boots she looked up into his face. There must have been a photo shoot in progress for his face seemed powdered and there was a hint of brown eyepencil on his lower lids. He seemed preoccupied and cross.

The royal family was not infrequently seen at Dizin. People knew they were there by the helicopters that would be touching down and lifting off all day. But oddly enough Roya never encountered them on the slopes. On the way up on the gondola one day she caught a glimpse of the queen, flanked above and below by members of her entourage. Roya turned back to follow her majesty's cautious and correct slalom down the slope. Perhaps the presence of the royal family was carefully choreographed to shield them from being observed if they took an unglamorous tumble on the slopes. Surely the king of kings could not risk being observed by his subjects if he wiped out on the slopes. Though, sadly, in a few short years the whole world would witness a much deadlier wipeout.

On one rare occasion Roya's mother had accompanied them on a ski day. She did not ski so she stayed inside the lodge all day by the fireplace. Reading her book she noticed from the corner of her eyes that the lodge was suddenly emptied and the queen and her kids were ushered in. Roya's mother must have looked innocuous for nobody asked her to leave. At some point the younger prince started poking at the fire in the fireplace. Roya's mother looked up disapprovingly from her book and in the blink of an eye a French nanny rushed to contain the unruly prince. This is the prince who years later would put a bullet through his brains in Boston, a few years after his younger sister died of drug overdose in London—events that would require the former queen to conjure up the strength to absorb the shock that would have otherwise led to more family tragedy. It turned out the strength had been honed in her by surviving betrayal and grief of epic proportions.

One guy who was not interfered with in the queen's presence was Stanislav Fiaper, the older of the Russian Fiaper brothers. These remnants of the white Russians who had found their way to Iran were outsiders to all groups who frequented Dizin. But of all the people there it was these misfits who should have commanded more interest than they did. They were not young and handsome but they were not as old as they appeared either. The older, taller Fiaper had the reputation of being a good skier but he was rarely seen on the slopes. He mostly hung out in the lodge, getting drunk on the vodka that people bought him. He started in the morning, smelling progressively more strongly of alcohol as the day wore on, and generally acted as a kind of buffoon. But there was something endearing about him. Nobody knew where he lived or what he did but he somehow managed to dress well and hang out with rich people. At any rate, Fiaper was a mainstay at Dizin and everyone teased and liked him, and some even said the queen herself was protective of him. Perhaps she took pity on him as a victim of the Russian revolution. If that was the case she was more prescient than the rest of us. Back in Dizin we were the equivalents of nineteenth-century Russian upper classes. But while in real-time our Russian counterparts were living the nightmare of the next phase, we were still taking troika rides in our furs.

(Drink up Stasik, drink up.)

It would be decades later when Roya would encounter Stanislav Fiaper in San Francisco, where he had joined other white Russian émigrés, many of whom had fled to the U.S. via Vladivostok and China. But by now Fiaper felt closer to the émigrés of the revolution in Iran, though his Russian was still better than his Persian. He invited Roya and family to his little dank apartment on Otis street and served them Russian delicacies accompanied by crisp pickled cucumbers and Roya's dad's favorite, spicy Russian mustard. And of course lots of vodka. He offered his services to outfit Roya and friends with proper ski gear, complete with discount from a buddy's sports store. But alas, at that point, skiing was out of everyone's budget. None of them had skied in years.

But a few years before the revolution Roya's life went through a personal upheaval. Within a year her brother and a number of their friends were shipped off to boarding schools abroad–the inflexible rigor of Iranian schools made a foreign education appear more manageable for unconventional kids. The worst blow to Roya was Katti's departure to an English boarding school. Roya accepted the unraveling of her world the way children accept things that are out of their control, with confused resignation. The year that she was completely alone in the back of the Land Rover was the year that she did badly in school. Having declared a math major (kids in Iranian schools had to choose majors in tenth grade) and not being up to snuff, Roya had a tutor who came to her house to work with her on math. This guy, Ahmad, was the son of one of her dad's colleagues, a smart guy on a mission. Batool, Roya's family's housekeeper (their *kaargar*, "worker," as she called herself), did not like this guy. She would come and sit in a corner while Roya and Ahmad studied at the dining table. Batool peered at this guy with intense distrust; she never did that with any other male friend. It turned out her instincts were correct. Ahmad had given himself the task of recruiting Roya to his cause, which as far as anybody could gather had to do with "armed struggle," some version of a Bolshevik revolution.

Roya was curious. Bookworm as she was, she asked for reading suggestions. "The Little Black Fish," he recommended. That was a children's book by a radical Azarbaijani author who had drowned in the Aras river a few years back. It was rumored that SAVAK did it. (Decades later it was revealed that the rumor was spread by another radical writer.) Roya said nothing about the ridiculous suggestion of a children's book. "I've already read that," she said. "Read it again," Ahmad said authoritatively. You've got to be kidding, Roya thought–and she tested him: "But I read more sophisticated books than that," she said. Ahmad took off his glasses, set them on the table and hissed: "People who read more *sophisticated* books"–he made a mocking face as he said the word– "should be sent to dig ditches." The gulag, labor camps– Roya had heard about those and she wasn't interested.

But not everyone wanted to send her to dig ditches. On her way home after school Roya had gotten into the habit of stopping by a bookstore where she eventually made friends with a young man who worked there. This guy, Reza, was a university student who loved passing on good books to her. He wore thick-lensed glasses and had a way of holding books in his hands as if he was about to devour them. Any ideological bubble that Ahmad tried to blow for Roya, Reza popped with subversive fiction: *Rust, Opinions of a Clown, Moderato Cantabile, The Stranger*... Once after school she ran to the bookstore to discuss Oriana Fallaci's *Nothing, and so be it*, which was just hot off the press. She was proudly holding her glossy copy when Reza set her straight. "Fallaci is shallow and sensationalistic," he quipped. "You can do better than her." Roya did not compare herself to Fallaci but she was deeply flattered. Between Batool and Reza she was safe.

She was safe but she was lonely, especially on the slopes. She took turns riding in the chairlift with her dad and her uncle, brothers who could not have been more different. Roya's dad was a serious man who had the sardonic air of someone who knew too much. He was no fun. His younger brother, the great favorite Amu Jamsheed, on the other hand, was a cross between Dean Martin and Mary Poppins. He had quit school when he was sent to the U.S. to study and had become a professional ballroom dancer. When he had returned to Iran after twenty years of drinking and partying in California and Colorado, he lived with Roya's family. He lifted the spirit of the household and was the favorite among all the kids. He was lighthearted, playful, and never lectured. He was the one who started them skiing and told them about Aspen and Winter Park.

Roya did not want to hurt her dad's feelings but she always preferred to ride with her Amu Jamsheed. He told so many stories. He had danced with Marilyn Monroe in LA; she was a natural, he said. He had danzoned till dawn in Batista's Cuba; cha cha cha and mambo are great fun, but danzon is witty, he said. He mimicked the exaggerated gestures of paso doble and told how when the first solo-guitar notes of Malgueña sounded everyone cleared the floor for those who could really pull off a paso doble–like him! He took off his glove and tapped the rhythm of different steps on the chairlift bar. Roya had spent a lot of time watching him do the same thing on the steering wheel of his Peykan, absentmindedly humming and rapping with his ring that had a cracked stone embossed with the head of Alexander the Great. "Step, step, step-side-together…" he had tried to teach Roya and Katti to tango in the living room. He spent hours explaining the intricacies of samba to the girls–but he needed more than a couple of awkward kids, barefoot on the living room carpet. Eventually he gave up dancing or trying to teach it. At any rate, playful as he was it was simply beyond his ability to provide the companionship Roya needed in her friends' absence.

Roya had her friends in school and had made her first non-family friend, Reza, after school but she skied mostly alone. She eyed kids her age at Dizin. A sweet Austrian girl named Elisabeth persistently smiled at her, probably because she was even lonelier than her. She was the kid sister of a tall stern-looking guy who drove a hot BMW 2002 that Roya checked out from the corner of her eyes. But the friendship did not develop much beyond smiles. Elisabeth mainly spoke German and Roya could only speak in the English she had learned from the dust covers of rock and roll albums. Communication was rudimentary.

Most of the other kids at Dizin were those that Roya secretly looked down on. They were the taqooti kids who went to foreign schools and studied in English, French or German. Perhaps their parents thought that literacy in Persian was not necessary for their kids, that their brilliant futures lay somewhere much grander than good old third-world Iran. Among these parents were of course those who not being sufficiently taqooti themselves scrambled to pay the high tuition of international schools for the opportunity to throw their kids into the company of high taqoot. These foreign language-educated kids, even though they spoke Persian, did not impress Roya at all. She had a few distant friends in that set and judged them harshly for not being literate enough in Persian. She was particularly appalled at their penmanship which was on the level of kids who went to Iranian elementary schools. Iranian kids were taught calligraphy from an early age and by the time they were in high school they were experimenting with writing in full adult *shekasteh* script. Roya had a particular fondness for penmanship classes, dipping reed pens in the clumps of silk thread saturated with black ink, practicing the flowing strokes of the *nasta'liq* script. She loved the subdued chatter as the whole class was lost in a cacophony of squeaking pens and piles of stained paper. Inevitably the din of

the chatter would grow loud and the eccentric calligraphy teacher immersed in trimming reed pens, would look
up from his well-worn pocketknife, and rap the desk with
uncut reeds: "Quiet, ladies. Quiet."

The year of the failing math classes Roya had
been particularly intrigued by her Persian Literature
teacher. She dictated to them a whole text book of grammar and literary analysis. She discoursed on literary
tropes and gave examples from poems that were already
familiar to the students. Roya kept this text and used it
as a reference in graduate school. To explain s*ahle mom-
tane'*–"impossible simplicity"–she gave this famous Sa'di
poem as an example:

> *A drop of rain fell from a cloud,*
> *It was put to shame by the vastness of the sea:*
> *For where there is the sea, what am I?*
> *If it is then I am not.*

The drop of rain, humbled to nothingness by the great-
ness of the sea, was eventually transformed into a pearl
worthy of kings. Roya knew this poem from second
grade when she had memorized it to compete for a prize.
She had not won the prize but never forgot the poem.
It was Sa'di's version of "to be or not to be"–not wondering about the efficacy of suffering slings and arrows
but ruminating on how being is achieved by humbling
oneself to the point of nonbeing. The magic was that he
expressed it in the simplest possible language, humbling
himself–as great a master of language as ever was–before
language itself, as it were. Now Roya's teacher was trying
to show her students how it was that the art of poetry can
achieve the impossible simplicity of being itself.

Just the other day Roya had walked among the

fig trees and potted Yas plants in her yard, carrying her handwritten text book, studying for a quiz. She had read the lines her teacher had used as examples over and over again. She had tried to understand. Then she had wondered if she should have declared a literature major instead of mathematics. But literature was old-fashioned; math was modern. And yet, her math homework already done, she found that thinking about poetry had no end. Poetry bewildered her—and gave her a headache. When it got dark she went inside, needing to let off steam and clear her mind. She put on Jimi Hendrix. No one had told her it could not or should not be done. She turned up the volume and closed her eyes. She was transported and her headache lifted.

One cold and sunny day at Dizin Roya went inside the lodge to warm up. "Hey Jahanshah…" someone yelled and Roya turned around to look. She caught a glimpse of a bearded young man who waved to his friends and ran outside to catch up with them. Thus it was that "Jahanshah," King of the World, entered Roya's life. He became her imaginary companion on the slopes. But first, however, he went through some changes. Roya did not have a taste for older men (like guys in their twenties) or facial hair. Her Jahanshah was her own age with smooth cheeks and black eyes smiling at her from behind the beanie pulled down over his brow and his turtleneck unfolded over his nose. He waited for her as she slowed down to negotiate the moguls. He raced her schussing down to the lower lift. He rode with her on the chairlift, sharing the army blanket that the lift attendants handed out on particularly frigid days. She talked to him incessantly. She explained *sahle motane'* to him, expressing her own views on it. She discussed the relative merits of Led

Zeppelin and Pink Floyd, and told him why she liked Carlos Santana the best. She conversed and laughed with him, hummed songs to him, and stopped bugging her uncle to ski with her.

On a dark and gloomy day in midwinter, when small persistent snow flakes had been coming down for a while, a major storm threatened the ski area. The slopes were emptying fast, everyone leaving to head back to the city before the roads closed. But the locals were not convinced of an imminent storm so, keeping a watchful eye, they kept the lifts running. Roya rushed to get one last run in before closing. The lift operator, heavily wrapped in icicled woolens, pulled the swaying chair toward her and gave the snow accumulating on the seat a swipe. Roya grabbed the blanket that he handed her, got on, and waved thanks. She wrapped herself in the coarse and stiff blanket, leaving just a slit open for her eyes.

It was bitterly cold. She took turns holding the blanket with one hand, keeping the other warm between her legs. The tiny sharp flakes blurred her vision and stung the little skin that was exposed of her nose. The mountains were silent and empty. The only sign of human life was the whirring and rattling of machinery and the clanging of metal against metal as the chairs cleared the poles in regular intervals. Roya watched the clumps of dry snow that flew off the descending chairs with every jolt and she felt the propulsion of the powerful engine that carried her up the mountain. The cold was stinging and the lack of visibility unnerving. To fight off the loneliness and fear creeping up on her she pulled the blanket away from her face and squinted to catch a glimpse of the sky through the sheet of falling snow. The sky was dark and distant but it was not entirely invisible. She

wiped the snow off her goggles and breathed the cold air
in. It sent a sharp chill through her chest.

To distract herself she tried to conjure up Jan-
hanshah or think of a song, but anything she tried to
imagine felt forced. She gave up and listened to the silence engulfing the clamor of the chairlift. She noticed
that the din and clatter of machinery was nothing compared to that vast silence. It was a silence that seeps inside your head and takes over. Her mind became as white
as the landscape and she succumbed to the nothingness.
Then eventually, from the depths of memory, the voice
of Janis Joplin rang in her ears. You don't play Janis in
your head, you certainly can't sing along with her, you
just feel her. Roya felt the resonance of the notes that
Janis belted out. She felt the sharp shrieks of the elec-
tric guitar slashing through her dissonant chords. She let
Janis's weightless upper register, floating in and out of
hearing range, wash over her. Janis Joplin is one of those
musicians who make you hear notes that they don't actually play or sing, almost like they imply melodies. She
revealed things to Roya about herself that eluded her.
And when all hell broke loose in her voice and her band,
Janis's unsung melodies clashed with the emphatic blasts
of her drummer's downbeat. It was pure fire. The burn-
ing of ice.

Never resist Janis, Roya thought, let her carry you
up and away. Which is what the chairlift did. Just as the
air around her grew the darkest and the sheet of falling snow the thickest, the lift pierced through the storm.
At eleven-thousand feet the sky brightened. The fury of
snowflakes let up. Roya uncovered her face and looked
over her shoulder below at the slabs of cloud she had just
cleared. As she reached the top of the lift the sky cleared

to a crisp blue. She slid off the lift and glided until the fresh powder stopped her. She stood still for a moment. Then she stamped her feet to pack the powder under her skis and wiggled her toes inside her frigid boots. She blew warm air into her gloves and took a look around. The solemn look of the distant peaks brought a wide grin to her face. The slope beneath her was clear for a long stretch but a blanket of buttery clouds spread over the lower peaks. She would ski down through it. She knew every turn down the mountain. Cold air, warm muscles, and the impending rush of speed made her heart skip a beat. Before she gave herself a push with her poles she took one last look at the awesome expanse that stretched all around her, and she knew that the excitement of foreign books and music notwithstanding, this was the greatest place on earth. And she was the king of the world.

GOOD LUCK IN GHANA

I was struck by it the minute I walked in. The resemblance!

There was no comparison of course. Jamma was much taller and darker. He had a long and narrow-shouldered shape with the slight hunch that many tall people are prone to. He moved with a touch of trepidation. He was much too reserved–all of this the opposite of Francisco.

But it happened the minute I caught his eye. I can't say there was recognition; you can't recognize someone in someone else. But there I stood frozen, glaring at him, searching hungrily for that which was not there. But there also *was* something there. And that's what made me lose my presence of mind and forget my business.

I stammered something to the effect that "Maryam F suggested that I get immunization updates from you." A couple of years ago we had worked with him on another project and somewhere in my files I must still have the version of the text with his editing on it. But at that time I did not meet him.

He leaned over his desk, smiling, and I didn't

know whether Maryam had already explained what I needed and I was repeating myself and should cut it short, or to go on. I needed material for human interest stories that tugged on people's heartstrings and loosened their purse-strings; I worked in fundraising at Unicef HQ in the mid 1990s. But it was really the smile swimming in Jamma's eyes that distracted me. I recognized Francisco's smile, though the quickness and the edge were missing. But what was the occasion for this smile? Was he "recognizing" me?

"What is it you're looking for?" he asked. "Immunization campaigns? Coverage figures? Constraints? Funding?"

"Stories," I said, "whatever has narrative value."

Story…? I'll tell you a story.

Life offers occasions through which the space of one's existence is doubled. I borrow the phrase from Jean-Jacques Rousseau when in his old age he wished for no more than the pleasure of reading his earlier writing. But the occasion may present itself as a man. The occasion—*he*—may knock on the door and walk in.

Maryam S and I were in the backyard when Francisco ran down from the second-floor apartment he was subletting, to tell us that some ungodly character was lurking in our backyard. It was the summer of 1984 on the Upper Westside in New York City and my ground-floor apartment had already been broken into twice.

After that day we became friends and one time Francisco tacked a poem, "I be kool, something something something" on my bookshelf, and gave me that swimming smile of his. He was at his peak. Everybody was in awe of him. In the mornings we walked to Columbia campus together, he to his bar review class and I to my summer work-study job at the Middle East Institute. He studied, took the bar, and passed it so effortlessly that I had no idea any of that was hard to do.

Once I came home to find him sitting on the banister outside our brownstone, his legs dangling, smoking a cigar, like the suave Puerto Rican gent that he was. Normally he did nothing Puerto Rican. He even preferred to call himself black rather than Puerto Rican. He hardly used his Spanish and when he became a practicing corporate lawyer he dressed in $1,000 dress shirts from UK and was only to be seen at Carnegie Hall, a few upscale jazz joints, and the Yale Club. I called his taste pretentious and unimaginative, and he called me a hard woman.

But there was one episode that jabs at me now. In the early days of our friendship the wife of a friend commented that Francisco looked like a rapist. We were all graduate students at Columbia but Francisco already had a PhD from Yale and a law degree from Harvard. He called any even slightly radical comment "vituperative." Once I gave him a present of a framed Iranian stamp commemorating the taking of American hostages and he called me "vitriolic." "Another V word?" I asked, and he gave me a sideways glance through his "spectacles." For God's sake, the guy was a golden boy straight out of an Ivy League yearbook.

Rapist? Was it the dark skin? Was it the glint behind the smile? Was it that he tread some holy ground not belonging to his kind? Well, that was the end of my friendship with that husband and wife and I thought no more of it. I thought the comment forfeited any discussion or explanation as to why I did not want to see them again. But now I am troubled that it did merit the thought that I did not give it.

"I am conflicted," Francisco would say to me. "I run on sadness and fear."

But know, Gentle Reader, that these were comments he made to shut out a conversation not to open one. And they were made if you said that he had a drug habit. "Weekends are my own," he said. "I can do blow all day and listen to Miles."

He died of an overdose, heroin and morphine, at age forty-one. He had finally been refused partnership in the illustrious law firm where he worked. It did not help that the WASPiest bank in town gave him a posh job in Hong Kong. He had been rejected by the club that he coveted.

"I'll give you what I have," said Jamma. He stood for a moment before his bookcase, then pulled out, one by one, journals and bindings.

"Press release on measles eradication in Haiti, case studies of TB in AIDS patients, diphtheria resurgence in NIS countries."

Dip-theria—he enunciated extra clearly. He took his seat and rested his elbows on the desk. "For the latest on the dip-theria resurgence talk to Stephen." He jotted down Stephen's extension number on a piece of paper and handed it to me.

Now the smile was playing at the corners of his mouth. I recognized this too. But his smile lingered whereas Francisco's would start to quiver after a moment and burst into a semi-suppressed chuckle.

"I'm giving you all my originals because Maryam sent you," he said, and then his smile finally widened in recognition. "My daughter's name also is Maryam." I smiled. Years ago my Arab professor had coyly mentioned that his wife's name was Maryam. At the moment I was on my way out of his office and I pretended not to hear.

There are so many Maryams. I met Maryam F at work. Maryam S and family I've known all my life and for a while she and I were roommates. To distinguish us people called us Maryam S and Maryam P. When we were children we were called Maryam #1 and Maryam #2; I was older so I was #1. I'm glad she was with me the day Francisco knocked on the door and walked into my life. He accompanied us to the backyard to investigate. A very dark-skinned man in black clothes was sprawled against a massive chunk of black stone—what the isle of Manhattan is made of—that apparently no one had found economical to remove from the linked backyards of a row of brownstones.

"It's a jungle out there," Francisco famously declared. Maryam S later commemorated that day by making a print for me by that title.

Jamma kept piling up information for my use. He would spring up and fetch something more: more recent, more interesting, more detailed. There was hardly a need for me to ask. I just watched him. I watched the twitch of every muscle in his face. I watched his hands. I hungered for the resemblance. I watched his every move, which was not at all like Francisco. I can't quite describe how Jamma moved. He moved the way he pronounced "dip-theria," proper and stiff beyond the call of duty.

Francisco had a bounce in his step that he played up or down at will. He didn't dance often but when he did he puckered his lips, closed his eyes and still managed to smile through them . His movements were in the feet and the hips. What he had was the Latin sway and not the African tilt.

And, boy, the Latin nerve!

Once Maryam S nervously told me that one day in the street Francisco had reached for her hand and said, "I love Maryam but I lust after you too." Poor Maryam S, she felt so bad she had to report it to me!

I laughed. I still laugh. There was nothing vulgar about Francisco. He was not a dandy. Try as he might.

When later I caught a glimpse of Jamma walking down the hall he was holding his head a little to the side, his shoulders pulled up, looking down at his feet. He walked like a suppressed crab. How unnecessary, I thought. You should not let anybody do this to you.

"They hired him with the promise to make him a P-5"–the UN ranks its professionals–so he turned down another offer and moved his family to New York. "He's the most knowledgeable one around here but now once again they're displacing him, to Ghana this time. And P-5 is out of the question."

"Do I love Francisco but lust after this man too?" I asked myself.

"I wish," I answered myself.

Alas, alas… how does one describe loss? He who expands the space of your existence by his, diminishes your life by his absence.

The poet says: *come to me in dreams, that I may live/ my very life again tho' cold in death.* Or, come to me in the smile, the bearing, the hands, the audacity.

Perhaps good old Jean-Jacques got it right again. Perhaps your existence is doubled in writing.

"Goodbye," said Jamma. "Hope I gave you enough for a story."

"Goodbye," I said. "Good luck in Ghana."

SINCE THERE IS NO HELP

I walk down two levels to catch the #2 train to Manhattan at the Grand Concourse subway station. A group of hollering teenage boys storm up the stairs, taking three at a time. I flatten myself against the railing to get out of their way. On their trail a very young mother with carefully painted lips and a far-away look in her eyes slowly makes her way up the stairs. She pulls a child behind her by the forearm—the little boy has to climb the stairs sideways not to fall backwards.

I teach English Composition to City University of New York freshmen at Lehman College in the Bronx. Since I've started teaching I pay closer attention to young people; I have to learn from them how to teach. But there is another reason why my attention lingers on young people. I look for something in their faces, their words, their movements, that would indicate to me that they are survivors, that they will *make it* to college.

I read student essays regularly. I have had students who write about sleeping in subway cars at night, about living in neglected buildings where after school one day they may discover the ruin of their families' belongings by

a collapsed ceiling or a broken water main. I have read
students' worries about younger siblings who are being
lured into drug dealing, about the hard decisions involved
in virtually single-handedly raising younger siblings. The
list really does go on. But obstacles must be overcome,
the hiking CUNY tuition has been paid, and our students
struggle to stay in school. They have become accustomed
to an education that is begrudgingly offered them. But
being a survivor is becoming costlier by the minute.

I am on my way home from a long day at school.
At the Grand Concourse station there is not much to take
one's mind off hardship. I look at the opaque, bluish pools
of something liquid covered with oily spots standing here
and there in the tracks. I follow the small gray mice flying
from one small heap of something to another, leaping into
hiding with the sound of an approaching train and darting
into view again when it leaves. I think to myself that it must
feel good to be so light.

The sound of a muted but crescendoing chord
reaches my ears. It is a harmonica. I can't see who is playing
but the sound is coming from the opposite platform. The
player is very experienced; he knows the acoustics of the
place. If he played any louder the echo would distort the
sound. He holds each chord without vibrato. The tempo
is very slow and the melody singing on top is sustained
carefully. Only at the end of a phrase does he introduce
a little tremolo, the wavering of the breath when it must
renew itself. The music rings in the air. The player knows
the architecture of the station and calls to it to play. The
underground tunnel responds. The harmonica falls silent
as the tunnel plays back its echo. Then there is a split
second of total silence after both sound and echo have
spent themselves, and before the next phrase begins. The

sound is soft but it takes on the whole space. People pace the platforms quietly. We all listen.

When my train comes I'm sorry to leave, but also relieved as usual. I am particularly tired on this day. Between classes I have attended a forum sponsored by the Student Council to inform students on the changes in store for the City University system—the "consolidation" plan, it is called. The proposal is to "consolidate" the resources of the various campuses of the City University of New York. It is early 1990s. A chancellor is hired who is best at carrying out certain definite policies of indefinite consequence. ("It's a dirty job but somebody has to do it.") What the new plan amounts to is the elimination of many departments and faculty members at individual colleges, so that in pursuit of their majors and interests students will have to commute to different campuses in different boroughs.

At the forum there is talk of the transportation costs of the average student commuting between campuses. There is talk of the evening student and the student with family responsibilities—can they afford the extra time that commuting requires? There is talk of work schedules—the majority of our students work almost full time. One of my best students works in a movie theater on 34th street in Manhattan and rides his bike home to the Bronx around midnight to save subway token money. On a salary of four-dollars-something an hour the price of a token is considerable. His first class in the morning is at 7:55, but the bike ride is short. Should he be prepared to ride to Queens next year?

There are more than commuting concerns, however. The plan is to change our campus to concentrate on nursing and physical education. We will no longer be a liberal arts college. "They are trying to stamp out all intellectual activity in the Bronx," a student comments. The assault on the worth of humanities is not new, but it has different meaning in different contexts. Community, history, cultural survival—the very subjects of humanities—acquire additional meaning for a population of mainly minority students. It is this relevance that has a life of its own independent of any CUNY chancellor and her plans.

As my train dashes and jolts along I think of the ride last night. An old black woman with her gray hair in loosened dirty corn rows walked through the subway car. She was dressed in a battered overcoat and old sneakers without laces. She had no socks, and underneath the coat her clothes were scanty. Outside, the wind blew so cold it sapped your strength. She held a paper coffee cup, darting her absent glance around and muttering to herself. A button she was wearing on her coat read: Respect and Protect the Black Woman. When I put a dollar bill in her cup she directed her glance at me and muttered to me for a second.

"Respect...?" I thought, "What respect?" She left our car for the adjoining one and the door banged after her. I suddenly went mad: "Who is it you are asking to respect you? The same people who snatched your children from you? Who put your men in shackles? Protect you for what purpose? You're not even needed any more. Your labor is superfluous. You and your men and your children are just extras now—extra mouths to feed."

Tonight I think about the consolidation plan. I think about my own career at CUNY. I am a part-time "adjunct," which means that for the same teaching load I get paid, at best, one-fourth of the salary of my full time colleagues—and I'm not even comparing myself to senior tenured faculty. Adjuncts teach something like 60 percent of the courses at CUNY. The saving adds up. As academic job opportunities have permanently dwindled, the adjunct faculty has swelled with over-qualified members. It is assumed that adjuncts are of two kinds: those who are in a sort of apprenticeship, and losers. If the former does not in good time land a full-time job somewhere—anywhere—it turns into the latter. It is not assumed that we *like* to teach at CUNY.

When I first started teaching at Lehman my very successful black Puerto Rican lawyer friend said that it was because I couldn't get a job anywhere else. The fact of the matter is that adjunct jobs are plentiful; you do have a choice. With or without this choice, however, we are perceived and treated as losers: a loser crew for a loser crowd. This same friend said to me: "You know that your students will never make it. They don't know how hard it is." Indeed, only a few of my students will "make it." I know and CUNY knows how hard it is; only very young people don't know. So we are hired to oversee the classrooms while students are in the transitional stage between admission and dropping out. We get paid as we do because, like our students, we are not worth the investment. Our labor is superfluous.

Between affirmative action and this new rage of "multiculturalism" we already lose many of our best students. Black colleges lose, and we lose. Like freshly ground pepper on an endive salad—a kindred eighties' phenomenon—our students tantalize the taste buds of politically correct college administrations. Our students' dark skin assuages the conscience of white administrations. Americans in general have an insatiable need to feel good about themselves.

But underneath this spectacle of integration

lie the ravaged communities from which these students come. The phenomenon is called brain drain, but these very young people don't know this either. And they don't know that the ravaging does not stop on the community level. They don't know that without a community your individual voice has no resonance, without a community you are flattened into cardboard. I should know; I've lived through a revolution. I've seen the before and after of the destruction of community. Now I am hired—for a pittance—to facilitate the destruction of other communities and pacify the members. At best, I am to help propel a student or two into a more promising future. The rest of my function is willy nilly. Teaching is not even relevant.

My successful lawyer friend, who paid dearly to climb to the heights of the American Dream, told me years ago that he despised the word "needy"—that's how he, the brilliant young boy, was described in his youth. I think of my train ride last night. I think of my charity towards that homeless woman. I think of a dollar bill. "Whose money is this?" I ask myself. After rent and basic sustenance, if any money is left I don't even want it. One dollar buys that old woman exactly what it buys me, and it doesn't buy either of us very much. My good will towards my students buys their good will towards me, and neither of our good wills gets either of us anywhere. I don't teach at CUNY from charity. I teach there because I don't feel inspired to teach endive salads, not for all the freshly ground pepper in the world. But the reality is that I don't even earn enough for rent and basic sustenance, let alone for paying back student loans. This is how it is that if I want to stay in the profession I will eventually have to leave CUNY to teach endive salads.

I go home to spend a little quiet time before sleeping.

I only have time to read a short story—Chekhov it shall be. "On Official Business" is the story of a young Muskovite coroner trapped in some obscure province. In his dream one restless night the village constable, an old man, and an insurance agent dead by suicide, a young man, sing to him: "We're marching, marching, marching along. You are warm, you have bright lights, you are comfortable, but we are striding into the icy cold and the blizzard, through the deep snow. We know no peace or joy, we bear all life's burdens, both ours and yours..." The world is twice removed from those days: once to the triumph in the name of those who bear all life's burdens—at least in Russia— and twice to this day. Now it's not at all clear who bears the burdens of life. If labor is burden, then it is neither the old black woman nor I—neither the village constable nor the educated Muskovite of Chekhov's time—who bear any burden. Our society does very well without the labor of both of us.

The next morning I also teach. I retrace my steps of last night to catch the #2 uptown. I pass a row of neglected but still sturdy brownstones. Some bird half flies half hops up the rusty fire escape zigzagging the side of the building. I catch one last breath of fresh air before descending into the underground again. Adjuncts do a lot of commuting.

When I step inside the #2 train, there are little flyers placed on the seats here and there. "Are you overcome with conditions that are not natural? Does bad luck seem to follow you?" The flyers are advertisements for astrology readings by Mrs. Yolanda: "$10.00 readings for $5.00." Located in a "Refine Area Upper West Side," Mrs. Yolanda offers her help: "I warn you gravely, suggest wisely, and explain fully." Things can indeed go very wrong in life. Mrs. Yolanda enumerates some: spells, bad luck, evil influence, separation, distress, change in a loved one, lost and stolen articles... What particularly strikes me, however, is the first trouble that the flyer mentions: unnatural conditions. People in the west have been wailing about unnatural conditions for quite a few centuries now. *This is not in my nature*—perhaps this is the ultimate cry of protest across culture, across history, across any kind of division right now.

At 125th Street I'm still looking at Mrs. Yolanda's ad, at the signs of the zodiac on it, at the xeroxed version of a painting of a ravishing woman with flowers and ribbons and beads in her long black hair. When the train takes off, the second it establishes its speed after the initial jolt, a chord is hit on a harmonica. It is held a fraction of a second longer than a staccato. I look up. A young black man standing in the back of the car, eyes closed, cups a harmonica with both hands. He starts playing.

The tunnel our train passes through is uneven. It widens and it narrows: the reverberation of the sound of the traveling train is diffused, then concentrated. In stretches the tunnel is supported by pillars: racing along these the train produces an evenly divided clamor. The train meets an oncoming one: the clamor is layered over with conflicting percussive intervals. The trains disengage each other at their tails: the crammed rhythm comes to an abrupt halt. The harmonica player is not playing the cantabile phrases of last night. He weaves in and out of the train clamor with sforzando snatches—splashing bucketfuls of sound against a backdrop of noise. The chords are accentuated evenly and broken off with the player's tightening of his hands around the harmonica. Melody is only hinted at. The player takes short, deep breaths.

    As he walks the length of the subway car he trails behind him on a rope attached to his back a crate containing his belongings, wobbling on make-shift wheels. His paper coffee cup is perched on top of the crate. I dutifully put some money in there and get off at 149th St., the Grand Concourse.

    Running up the stairs to transfer to the #4, I cannot take more than two stairs at a time. I'll do it while I can.

LOVE OF A GOOD MAN

If it had not been unseasonably warm for January it would have been a great day. The sun was shining and the air was clean and crisp. But most people were too warm and weighed-down by their heavy coats, which made them a little extra impatient and edgy. Leslie had just dropped something off and was ticking off items on her last minute to-do list, one by one. She was leaving the next day for Istanbul where her boyfriend had landed a teaching job at the American University. Scrambling down the stairs to the subway she literally bumped into an old friend.

"Azalea!" said Leslie.

"Leslie!" said Azalea.

The friends had not seen each other for a long time and although they were both in a hurry they exchanged phone numbers and promised to keep in touch.

Leslie's flight was the following evening on Austrian Airlines and she had an eight-hour layover in Vienna. She did not look forward to the long wait but she was resigned to it and stocked up with some good reading.

As it turned out, the long wait in Vienna did not

go that badly. Vienna airport was small and pleasant and civilized. As she settled herself down in its only cafeteria with a good cup of coffee and was fishing in her bag for a book, a tall and handsome young man approached her with a big smile on his face.

"I'll be damned if it's not Leslie Malone," he said. "God, it's been a long time."

Leslie recognized Peter Babbit. She and Leslie and Peter had gone to college together and while Leslie had occasionally had dinner with Azalea over the years, she had not seen Peter since graduation. Peter had missed his flight to New York City and had a long time to kill until the next one. He changed his mind about going into the city and stayed at the airport, keeping Leslie company.

"Talk about a coincidence," she said, setting down her cup of coffee that had gotten cold. "I don't see you and Azalea for so long and then I run into you one after another in two days."

"A double coincidence for me," said Peter. "I was wondering how I could get in touch with Azalea. I've been wondering how she's doing."

Peter and Azalea had gone to elementary school together and had met again in college. In fact, Peter used to be in a sort of love with her when they were children. They would hold hands and walk and Peter loved looking into Azalea's turquoise eyes. Sometimes he would even think about her beautiful eyes before falling asleep at night. But for such a romantic little fellow Peter grew up to take after his father and devote himself to making money. By the time he met up again with Azalea in college he had no time for anything soft and lovey-dovey. He quickly finished college in his small town and moved to a famous university to get his MBA. He hit Wall Street in 82.

It was one of those things: the right guy at the right time in the right place. Peter made a killing: six digit salary, enormous bonuses, and a couple of good apartments he bought and sold in the nick of time. For a man his age he was loaded. Plus, there was that nifty little inheritance winking at him in the future: the family business had grown into a successful state-wide chain.

But it was not all luck; Peter had been smart with his money. He had not lived the extravagant life of many yuppies of his generation. The crash of 87 left his personal finances relatively unscathed and he finished the decade practically able to retire. But the money he lost for his firm as a result of the crash opened his eyes to the perils of his profession. He was pretty shook up and took a big professional stumble. After he recovered from a near nervous breakdown he realized that the stress, overwork, and neglect of a certain part of himself was catching up with him. He also had the example of his father's early heart attack before him, so he made a radical decision to go into semi-retirement and enjoy life for a while. He decided to take a year off and travel and contemplate his life. This is what had brought him to Europe.

Six, seven months into the trip, and many big-city museums and small-town music festivals later, he was already getting bored. But Europe had inspired him. He wanted quality of life: leisurely days, good food and wine, stimulating conversation. He wanted to belong to a bigger international context while maintaining his American authenticity. He felt homesick but also energized to start a new life with time to spare—and culture and identity. He could afford it now.

A couple of days before his flight back home he

was deep in thought while taking a walk when the name Azalea popped into his head. It was as if some invisible hand with a magic wand planted it in there: Bing! He had heard that Azalea lived in New York and now suddenly he had a strong urge to look her up. It was uncanny to run into Leslie with Azalea's phone number handy. When Leslie finally boarded her flight to Istanbul, Peter went directly to a telephone and dialed New York.

When Azalea ran into Leslie in the subway she had been on her way to an interview. She was the one giving the interview, that is; Leslie had done well for herself professionally. After her BA she had stayed in her hometown college and pursued a PhD in English and Comparative Literature. The department was small but growing and they had loved her and taken good care of her with scholarships, grants, and RA- and TA-ships. She had whisked through the doctoral program in record time and hit the job market while there still were positions to be filled. In fact, she had had a choice and she had opted to relocate to New York for the experience. She had taken her present job as director of the composition program at a small private college in the city. Although the job was not quite in keeping with her specialization in comparative literature–19c. European novel, albeit in translation–she had taken it, viewing it as an academic stepping stone. Anyway, she felt she was still young and there was no reason not to give in to the lures of New York City.

Then came the great shining moment in literary studies and liberal arts in general: theory, criticism, theory of criticism and criticism of theory, post-colonial feminism, dialectics of diacritics, deconstruction of post-structuralism, and of course the hermeneutics of

Canon as Urtext... She had no training in any of this. Plus, the job market dried up. So Azalea gladly stayed on as Director of Composition Program in the small college and found all kinds of good things about it. She called herself a bread-and-butter kind of academic. Students are illiterate, she explained, and someone has to educate them. She scorned the fads and fashions of state-of-the-art literature departments. But having gone to graduate school in the late seventies and having missed out on the subversive discourse of academic revolutionaries she was not quite comfortable with the latest developments in the field. She scorned it all as fad but it still made her uneasy. She stopped going to MLA conferences. There was no need; she had a job. The 90s started on a secure note for her.

At any rate, she was on her way to interview an adjunct for teaching a composition class when she ran into Leslie. She got to her office only a few minutes before her appointment and the prospective adjunct was already waiting. She was a recent PhD, only a few years younger than Azalea, with a respectable amount of teaching experience. She was dressed in black leggings, a long sweater, and nice supple boots. There was nothing flashy or strained about her and she projected an air of ease. The straight and crisp cut of her hair made Azalea feel self-conscious about her own old perm frizzing the tips of her hair, and she thought the adjunct was under-dressed for a job interview.

They shook hands and took their seats. Azalea took out the adjunct's CV which she had scrutinized beforehand. "Comparative literature, right?" she began with a smile.

The adjunct had a PhD in comp lit from an Ivy

League university.

"There are no jobs in comp lit these days, are there?" Azalea continued.

The adjunct was aware that directors of composition programs often had more glamorous academic aspirations but the job market being what it was... So she took the question as a general conversation opener. "There are no jobs period," she said, " but the lack of jobs in comp lit, I think, is partly due to the fact that it's not quite clear what comp lit is."

"What do you mean by that?" Azalea was a trifle abrupt, remembering that she ought to be the one bringing up topics.

"Well, we were taught a lot of theory in grad school and I suppose theory does make literature comparative but comp lit has become too much of an esoterically practiced discipline."

"How do *you* define comparative literature?"

"I don't have a definition off hand," the adjunct had only herself to kick for starting this conversation, which she did. "I suppose a rethinking of the field is in order."

Her evasive comment made it clear that she was ready to move on to an interview for a basic composition class. Azalea sensed this and thought it preposterous that the adjunct should cue the moving on. Now she began the firing of questions she considered relevant.

"Tell me about your teaching experience. Have you done other things than teach remedial composition?" she asked.

The CV in front of her had full well informed her that the adjunct had taught remedial through advanced levels, as well as ESL. She had also taught literature humanities, western civ, as well a number of upper division seminars. But Azalea sort of felt like unnerving the adjunct.

"What would you say your students in all these classes have in common?" she asked as soon the adjunct had finished enumerating her experience.

"There is just too much educational inconsistency and cultural diversity for me to say…" the adjunct was racking her brain for something both accurate and *correct* to say. "With so many inner-city and immigrant kids here I would say what they have in common is being survivors and very motivated."

"But how would you define them as a student body?" Azalea was not ready to be pacified into reason.

"I have a tendency to become involved in each student's work a bit too individually, I'm afraid, to be able to generalize," the adjunct tried.

"They are not well read," Azalea revealed the correct answer.

"That depends on what you expect to find," thought the adjunct–some of us just take it for granted that Americans don't grow up reading. But she smiled and waited in silence.

"What sort of comments do you make on student papers in a composition class?" Azalea popped another hit or miss question.

"That depends on what each student is working on," the adjunct said. "If someone has literacy issues I correct their grammar and overlook questions of rhetoric in favor of a less damningly marked paper. If they are more advanced I comment on finer points."

"We always find something good to say on a student's paper here," again Azalea revealed the correct answer.

"Of course," said the adjunct. She had experience in many ways of defeating a high drop-out rate in her students, but she kept her silence again.

The adjunct's lapses into comfortable silence were provoking to Azalea. She felt that they put her on the spot; she had to quickly find something to fill them with. The interview dragged on and on and the adjunct was becoming less and less sure what the object of the interview exactly was. Finally there was a knock on the door and the interview came to an end.

"Is there the possibility of a second class?" the adjunct asked while putting on her coat. By this time Azalea was highly irritated. "Oh no–no, no. Not the first semester. I'll have to assess your teaching skills first."

When they shook hands goodbye Azalea said that she had to run the adjunct's CV by the Planning and Budget Committee which was meeting that same afternoon and would call her later in the day to inform her of the decision of the committee. There was no committee meeting of course; Azalea was just not quite prepared to be what she considered generous. After the adjunct left she collected her things and decided to call it a day. Leaving the ladies' room she caught a glimpse of herself in the mirror. She was dressed in her usual pleated skirt and button-down shirt that fell loosely over her hips. Neat pantyhose and pumps and she looked quite professional. She had learned to disguise her extra weight tastefully but any glance in any mirror and she immediately hated herself. She could never cross her legs and wrap them around each other the way the adjunct did.

At home she reflected that her mood had most definitely soured during the day. By the time it was time to go to bed she was having the old nagging thoughts: she had done well for herself professionally, especially compared to a lot of people in her profession, but... her life was just not complete. She needed a man in her life. This started her rehashing the deficiencies of old boyfriends: Roger was so insecure and he deserved those empty-headed glamour girls he went out with; and Michael, so egotistical and immature—and of course insecure, men are so afraid of educated and successful women, everybody knows this...

Azalea went to bed feeling defeated and bitter.

It seemed like she had just fallen into a deep sleep when someone gently tapped her on the shoulder. She opened her eyes to find a smiling woman standing over her. Her first reaction was to be afraid but the woman had such a calm and reassuring presence that Azalea only asked: "Who are you?"

"I am your fairy godmother," said the woman.

Azalea lost her wits for a second but quickly recovered herself. "What do you mean a fairy godmother?"

"You must have heard of fairy godmothers," she said. "Don't I look like one?"

The fairy godmother was a casually but nicely dressed older woman with twinkles in her eyes. She had a terrific head of gray hair cut short and straight, the kind of full, silvery hair that every woman says if she has when she gets older she won't color. There indeed was something striking about her: that knowing smile, that light touch, and especially those twinkling eyes were certainly out of the ordinary. "I want to have a little chat with you," she said. After Azalea had a chance to collect herself and put on a bath robe, they settled on comfortable sitting chairs.

"You see, fairy godmothers tend to work behind people's backs," the fairy godmother began. "They don't like to draw attention to themselves, so they do what they have to do behind the scenes. But I have a hypothesis that I want to test–which is why I made myself visible..."

"A hypothesis?" Azalea was curious.

"Yes. I think that operating in a sort of clandestine way creates dependencies. People become dependent on wishing for luck and for miraculous interventions. The extreme example is people who are addicted to lotto tickets: they spend their lives wishing for that one stroke of luck. So I've actually made a bet with some fellow fairy godmothers that if we make ourselves and the tricks of our trade known to people, they can take over our function. My hypothesis is that we can make ourselves obsolete–this will empower people and also free up some time for us to do things for ourselves instead of for others. By letting you in on what I've been up to I want to test my hypothesis."

"You mean you have been working on me–for me–whatever...?" Azalea asked.

"Yes, and you will find out soon enough. But I have designed the experiment such that the more you cooperate with me the more you are going to benefit. But you will have to make a pact with me."

"How can I trust you?"

"I'll give you a little advance, as it were. You sample your gain, think about it, and let me know."

"What kind of advance?" Azalea was beginning to show interest.

"Now, don't be shocked that as your fairy godmother I can read your thoughts. Weren't you sorely

missing having a man in your life earlier this very evening?"

"Go on."

"Well, I can send a really good one your way tomorrow. Tomorrow night I'll come back and ask if you
want to make a pact with me."

"Do I have a say in the choosing of this man?"

"You pick the form and I'll pick the content,"
said the fairy godmother. "Think about what you want
him to look like tonight and wait for tomorrow. Deal?"

"OK,' said Azalea, and watched the woman dis-
appear with a pleasant smile on her face.

Lying in bed for some time before falling back
asleep Azalea though that she must have had a ridiculous dream, but she went ahead and thought of what she
would want her man to look like anyway. She thought of
all kinds of combinations: blue eyes, dark eyes, curly hair,
straight hair, blond, black hair—each one had its own
charm. Finally she decided to leave the details to chance.
As long as he would be tall and handsome the specifics
didn't matter. She fell asleep, and the next day she was
excited in spite of her own constant reminders not to be
ridiculous.

When Peter Babbit called from Vienna airport
Azalea was not at home, so he left a message.

"Hello Azalea this is Peter Babbit. I hope you remember me. I ran into Leslie Malone in Vienna and she
gave me your number. I hope it's OK to call you. I'm on
my way to New York and I would love to see you," the
answering machine reported to Azalea's perked up ears.
She was a bit stunned. "Is this the advance the fairy godmother was talking about?" she asked herself in bewil-
derment. Her heart was beating fast. She felt confused,

but not confused enough not to remember that Peter was indeed tall and handsome, and that she had wanted to attract his attention in college to rekindle his old partiality to herself but had been unsuccessful.

Peter had been driven and uninterested, plus there were always more beautiful girls around. Her imagination started running wild. She tried to stop herself from daydreaming and fantasizing about Peter Babbit, but it was no use. "What if, what if, what if…" she kept asking herself. "What if something good really does happen between us?" She kept trying to keep her hopes in check but such strong desires were awakened in her that she was not equal to it. She impatiently waited for her fairy godmother that night and, sure enough, the woman with the twinkling eyes appeared to her again.

"Would you like something wonderful to come out of this reunion?" asked the fairy godmother.

"Is it really possible?" Azalea asked with enthusiasm despite her best effort to remain skeptical.

"Well, you've always considered yourself lucky, haven't you? Weren't you asked to your high school prom by one of the most popular guys in face of fierce competition? Didn't you snatch that four-year scholarship in grad school and sail without a single worry while others were taking out student loans? Weren't you even thinking yourself just yesterday when you were interviewing that adjunct that you were so lucky not to be in her shoes? Do you think nobody's been looking after you all these years?"

"Even if has been you all this time, why are you making yourself known now?"

"I told you that I'm experimenting. I want to see if self-knowledge can replace luck—*me*, that is. And the pact that I want to make with you is that you operate out of self-knowledge—which is to a large extent gratitude, really—and see if you need my interference again. I will give you a good man but you must give me the promise that you will commit yourself to understanding and appreciating what you have instead of operating out of hidden fears and insecurities and things like that…"

Azalea couldn't find anything wrong with the idea but didn't know what was specifically expected of her.

"The specifics might create some unpleasantness at first," the fairy godmother explained. "I have to give you a little eye-opening dose of self scrutiny to begin with. From then on you are to emulate the model yourself. Do we have a deal?"

Azalea thought there was nothing to lose; it certainly didn't seem like too high a price to pay for Peter Babbit. So she gave her consent and the fairy godmother began.

"Let's begin with what happened yesterday," she said. "You started out your day perfectly happily but somehow lost it all by the end of the day. Do you know what happened?"

"Some days are just like that. Maybe it was the change in the weather. Maybe it was the time of the month…"

"No. I'll tell you what happened. You resented that woman you were interviewing. It started with the way she looked. She had a nice body and a sense of style. You did notice, didn't you?"

"She was alright."

"She was well-dressed in a comfortable and unpretentious way. She was in good shape too, but neither the style nor the body should be grounds for envy. There was nothing special about any of it. With a little effort you can dress nicely and get in shape too. Why envy what you yourself can have…? Then again she had that Ivy League PhD and was probably well-versed in recent developments in the profession, that heavy stuff you have so much trouble with. She was competent and experienced and confident. Right?"

"She wasn't that experienced professionally. She should not have tried to dominate the interview," Azalea said. "And her answers were vague."

"Come now, you call it domination when she tried to get on to the purpose of the interview, which was not about literary theory but teaching a basic composition class? You know there is a difference between being interviewed for a bona fide academic position and a lowly adjunct job, don't you? Why should she subject herself to a drill for a position for which she is overqualified and that shamelessly exploits her? Be reasonable, the job barely pays over a thousand dollars for a whole semester."

"Her answers to my questions about teaching technique were vague," Azalea insisted.

"Your questions were general to the point of meaninglessness. What did you mean, how do you characterize your students' writing? It was perfectly legitimate that she had no single sweeping characterization to make. Or what did you mean about what kind of comments she makes on students' papers? She was trying to convey to you that she takes one student at a time. What's wrong with that?"

"OK, what are you getting at?"

"I'm trying to make the point that the poor woman had nothing to do with the souring of your mood. She said what she had to say, showed her competence, and should have been given the job. And you should have gone home relieved that you filled the position with a sensible person and thanked your own lucky stars that you are not in her situation. There was no reason to resent her and ruin your own mood–and I'll tell you why more specifically.

"Remember all those times when the PMLA comes and you look at it and promise yourself that you will read every single article and keep abreast of every single new book that is published in your field? Then all that daunting foreign language and all that endless jargon make you throw the journal aside and hate yourself? Remember how despite your most conscientious efforts issue after issue of PMLA collects dust and you keep postponing reading them? Well I'll tell you why you don't read those articles… It's because they're not worth reading. In fact, they are downright unreadable. Any normal person would rather flip through mail order catalogues than read the PMLA. There's no reason to hate yourself on this account.

"And I'll tell you another reason why you tend to get so foul-tempered. Remember those exclusive catalogues that are sent to you ever since you got your Platinum MasterCard? Remember the one with French lace curtains that made you so sad? You were thinking that you would never be able to afford real lace curtains, let alone the right kind of house to hang them in. You thought you would never experience a summer afternoon breeze through lace curtains of your very own. So in effect, you felt, neither the PMLA nor exclusive mail order catalogues were really yours. Remember how bitter that made you feel?"

Azalea was by now quite upset. "So why are you trashing me like this?" she asked.

"I'm not really trashing you at all. This stuff is what everybody secretly feels. I just want your acknowledgement on certain things so I can tell you the good news. For one thing, your hunch that this is an illiterate country and that all that academic hot air is really going nowhere is basically correct. The job you have is actually one of the few meaningful ones there are. Forget about the haunt and daunt of The Profession, upper case T, upper case P. Be straight with yourself. Who cares if you, or anybody, hasn't read it all? Everyone pretends to have done more homework than they have. Everyone is in secret awe of everyone else. No one feels they have quite grasped the coherence of their field. If people would not be so busy feeling inadequate they would realize there *is* no coherence to their field.

"Now, if you were smart you would enjoy what you've got. What's more, your power is in identifying with what it is that you do. You say that you're a bread-and-butter academic—well, then, believe it... And keep all this in mind in the upcoming days. I am here to let you know that I'm seeing to it that you will have reason to enjoy yourself a whole lot more than on account of your job. You can even have your French lace fairly soon. Peter Babbit is rich, you know."

The mention of Peter brought a flash of hope to Azalea's otherwise darkened consciousness. The discourse of the fairy godmother had unnerved her.

"And all this has to do with Peter Babbit?" she asked.

"Indeed it does," said the fairy godmother. "My

hypothesis is that if a person starts out from a strong position *and* proceeds to live her life with self-knowledge and
confidence then she will never need interference from a
fairy godmother anymore. So I will bring you and Peter
happily together–as a strong starting point–and if you
promise me that you will drop self-defeating strategies
that only ruin your mood I will find out if my hypothesis
is correct. Will you promise?"

"Whatever," said Azalea.

"Will you promise?" repeated the fairy godmother.

"Alright," Azalea finally agreed.

"Good. I won't come to see you for a while now.
Good luck." With this, the fairy godmother faded into
the air.

The next morning Azalea's mind was full of Peter
Babbit's merits. In a state of breathlessness at the prox-
imity of happiness, and with a heart ready for gratitude,
even if begrudgingly, Azalea thought she would now really keep a more generous disposition. She thought she
would give the fairy godmother's advice a try, but only
one step at a time. "If Peter calls me today and is excited
to see me, I'll call the adjunct and give her the job," she
resolved. Peter did call, his enthusiasm left nothing to be
desired, they made a date, and so the adjunct was hired.

Azalea was pleased with herself. She decided to
go ahead with a bit of makeover too, so she went out and
invested in an Itzak Miyake outfit complete with an an-
gular and drapey overcoat. She bought a matte lipstick,
and with the help of globs of styling gel she did her best
with putting her hair up in a tasteful chignon. She was
now ready to meet her promised man.

Peter was pleasantly surprised to find homegirl
so sophisticated, and a professor no less. She was not the

most beautiful woman he had ever met, but her blue-green eyes were still quite uniquely the color of turquoise and brought all kinds of vague, warm memories to his mind. At any rate, Peter was no longer hungry for pretty girls; he was into roots and substance now. He prodded her on and Azalea propounded on the challenges of educating inner-city youth and on literature and culture and art. She described to him the crisis in higher education, that in the face of dwindling budgets and the priority of the profession turning away from pedagogy, students were increasingly illiterate and in need of some serious teaching. Peter admired her "bread-and-butter" approach and felt that he now had a good grasp of the educational crisis. He was impressed that while he had to suffer a near nervous breakdown to learn to turn away from excessive materialism and unnecessary hype, she apparently had known this all along. Instead of getting involved in academic fashions she had gone in a direction that made a difference. She was idealistic and committed and confident. Her simultaneous existence in the worlds of high culture and down and dirty education intrigued Peter. She spoke well and eloquently. She knew a lot.

Of course, over time, they also talked about the old hometown and homefolk and "old fashioned" this and that. They hit it off indeed. And one thing leading to another they soon found themselves talking about living together and, in the spirit of Tradition–which they confessed they admired, despite their own secretly subversive lifestyles–marriage. For the time being Peter moved into Azalea's apartment where he spent his days indulging in the Penguin Classics volumes that Azalea had accumulated over the years. He discovered Stendhal and Turgenev and James Joyce. He read Chekhov short stories, a play by Kleist, and even *Pride and Prejudice* again. He could not wait for Azalea to get home to talk about all these wonderful things and making dinner together. They were very happy.

Love of a good man makes a woman lose unwanted pounds. In only a few month's time, Azalea thinned down to her desired weight and felt light and upbeat. She gave up on the idea of curls, cut off her hair that was frizzed from an old perm, and wore her fine blond hair in a stylish bob. She still dressed demurely for work, which Peter found unpretentious and attractive. He secretly thought that in a skirt and blouse and pumps she looked like an All-American Mom and he took pleasure in that. She treated the interestingly-fated adjunct she had hired kindly and occasionally spoke to her about pedagogic theory. In fact, she liked to engage the Ivy League PhD in professional conversation, and nonchalantly remark that she *hadn't* read this or that. It didn't bother her to admit to such things anymore; she had discovered a certain ironical tone. She felt on top of her game.

Spring found Peter and Azalea settled into a spacious central park-view apartment with lace curtains on order from France. They were quietly married at City Hall, with the festivities postponed for a summer reception at home.

Things were going splendidly and Azalea had never felt so happy. One spring day walking on her pretty block and taking in the splendor of the neighbors' azalea shrubs bursting in magenta bloom, she felt that she had never identified with her namesake flower as she did now. She felt that she too had hit her season of full bloomage. She now had everything she always wanted: happy marriage, good job, secure future. She felt good about herself and, catching sight of herself in people's windows, she thought she looked pretty good. She was on her way to work.

A busy day was ahead of her: a class to teach, office hours, a departmental meeting, and an interview. They needed a fresh adjunct to teach an extra composition class come fall semester; giving already-hired adjuncts more than one class was frowned upon by the administration because it strengthened adjuncts' hand in demanding health insurance benefits. She still hated interviews and wished she did not have to do the hiring but, on the other hand, she thought, it was worth the trouble. Being in charge of hiring allowed her to have control over the direction and focus of the department, its teaching philosophy, and its overall smooth operation. She felt that maintaining a friendly but rigorous atmosphere in her program was her responsibility. She felt equal to it.

The day went by pretty fast and before she knew it it was three o'clock in the afternoon and her interviewee was waiting outside her office door. Azalea greeted a young woman, well under thirty—an ABD, All But Dissertation. This new generation was only just beginning to make its presence felt in academia. Compared to even the generation that had gone to grad school in the eighties, these young people had early on accepted that they had to work very hard for a pittance. More and more classes were being taught by adjuncts while less and less job security was given to them. This young woman had only taught a course or two and was nervous and anxious for a job; thousand-dollars-a-semester was acceptable to her for the experience. She was also quite beautiful, Azalea suddenly noticed. The young woman had long natural curls in that alluring combination of dark charcoal streaked with silvery blond. She had gray eyes with dark lashes, which reminded Azalea of someone. She sat down, her cheeks a little flushed, and looked at Azalea expectantly.

"So... you haven't taught anywhere outside of your own department yet, have you?" Azalea began.

The prospective adjunct confirmed, then delivered a carefully rehearsed response about the good things that she had heard about teaching in this particular college and writing program. Azalea made a point of appearing untouched by the compliment.

"Tell me why you think you're qualified for this job," she said.

The young woman blushed some more and muttered things about her successful, if indeed limited, teaching experience, about caring about students, and believing in a good solid educational foundation. She was trying her best to articulate her approach of emphasizing reading in her classes and encouraging it by upping students' grades if they read any titles from her recommended reading list. She said that she found students not well read and believed that writing can best be learned by reading. Her earnestness shone through her frazzled nerves.

Azalea did not take her eyes off the young woman for an instant. She was both trying to test the interviewee's nerves and also to remember whom the woman reminded her of. The young woman went on, growing confused and more nervous, but Azalea did not break her silence. Finally the young woman stopped, unsure of whether she was expected to continue. She fidgeted in the silence that followed while Azalea maintained a stony stillness.

"What kind of comments do you make on students' papers?" she broke the silence, still without twitching a muscle.

"I think beginning writers need a lot of encouragement, so I always find something good to say before I critique them in any way," said the young woman. Then, after fearing she might have appeared a bit too touchy-feely, she added, "But I do emphasize a high standard of rhetorical rigor in the class."

"Anna Karenina," sparked Azalea's memory. "Her gray eyes remind me of Anna Karenina. Though she is younger and not at all as interesting."

The young woman was now feeling the strain of the interview. "I'm probably a really lousy teacher and it shows," she thought. Aloud she said, "I would really welcome the opportunity to become a better teacher, to learn from experienced faculty in this department."

Azalea pored some more over her CV. The young woman had grown up and gone to school in Europe and spoke fluent French and Italian, and read in German. "She reads her novels in the original language," Azalea noted.

"Your contact with American students is limited to your time in grad school, isn't it?" she asked.

"But I *am* American," the prospective adjunct said, "and I'm close in age to my students. I don't feel much distance..." And she stopped herself abruptly. She didn't want to appear to be calling Azalea old. "Blunder, blunder, blunder," she said to herself and bit her lips invisibly.

"A *young* Anna Karenina," Azalea was starting to have the old bitter taste in her mouth. Although the unassuming young woman bore no real resemblance to that exquisite fictional character, Azalea could not get over the gray eyes. This woman was young and would probably make an excellent, committed composition teacher, working three times as hard as a more seasoned faculty member. Azalea knew this. This woman was beautiful and young and cosmopolitan and probably had a good life ahead of her. This woman did not need Azalea's helping hand to give her career a jumpstart. Azalea was dedicated to excellence and experience in her staff. "Why should I give her free training?" was her thought.

Azalea got up to signal the end of the interview.

"Your qualifications are promising but I'm afraid we're looking for someone with more experience," she said. She was being generous, she thought. She could have chosen to keep the young woman waiting and hoping and feeling anxious, checking her answering machine every minute for the results of a committee meeting.

The young woman looked down, nervously smoothing the wrinkles in her simple linen suit. It was the only one she had. "I understand," she said, clearly disappointed. She bent over to collect her belonging and when she stood up to shake Azalea's hand the extra inches in her height made them both uncomfortable. After she left Azalea took out her pocket mirror to freshen up and noticed that with age one shows signs of fatigue more quickly.

That night when Peter was out with old Wall Street cronies, Azalea's fairy godmother appeared after her long absence. At her sight Azalea felt indignant.

"What happened? Why did you lose it again Azalea?" asked the fairy godmother. "You have everything you could want. Why did you suddenly feel so threatened by that young woman today?"

But Azalea was determined not to have any of it.

"I don't know who you could possibly be," she said to the fairy godmother. "I have thought about this for a while and I think you are just a figment of my own imagination."

"So what if I am?" asked the fairy godmother. "It only proves my point that you've always had everything you need."

"Well, I'll have you know that I am in control of my own life now. Which means that not only am I in control of the policies and standards of my department but I am also in control of my own imagination."

"So what if you are?" repeated the fairy godmother. "What does it matter if it is I who points out to you where you go wrong, or it is you yourself?"

"Don't play these games with me anymore," Azalea blurted out. "I am in charge of my own decisions."

The fairy godmother was silent for a moment. "Indeed you are," she muttered almost to herself. "Indeed you are."

She continued to look at Azalea with curiosity for a while. Her eyes shone more with discovery now than twinkle with playfulness.

"I see that I can't test my hypothesis in your case," she finally broke her silence. "Actually it looks like I lost my wager with the other fairy godmothers, but I did learn something…"

"I'm not interested in your speculations," Azalea barked again.

The fairy godmother was slowly fading from view. "I overlooked something essential in the design of my experiment. I did not make myself obsolete. I'm just not needed for the time being."

She took one last look at Azalea. "I should have known by now. Love of a good man makes a fairy godmother unnecessary."

And she was gone again, this time for good.

SHE'S NOT EXOTIC LIKE IRANIAN GIRLS

It was so nice to see Ashk. We were family friends, class-mates in fourth, fifth and sixth grades, and I had not seen him for a long time. I visited Ashk and his American wife in Maryland. He and I stood in the kitchen and talk-ed for a long time before joining the other guests outside on the patio. We talked about our old friends at Ashkan school (no relation!). We reminisced about Ashk's birth-day party, back in, oh, I think it was fifth grade. Sussan and I, and Goli and Nazanin were best friends at the time. A big part of being "best friends" back then was to be regular *leyley* partners. The four of us were mean *zizi* players, had our signature black travertine disks, and were accustomed to be playing some kind of game when-ever we were together. At the party the four of us, and I'm sure a few other girls, had been a bit unruly. We had a fabulous time running through the house (it must have been bad weather outside), over and under the staircase, and mercilessly banged the French doors. I ruined my fa-vorite party dress that night, the white one that had lace trims with tiny roses made from pink ribbon. Ashk had just received an instamatic camera for his birthday and we were a tad mean in frustrating him by not keeping still for a picture. Even back then I sensed that we were overdoing it.

Ashk and I talked about other friends. He told me that everyone thought I was so beautiful back then. What my beauty amounted to was that I had blond hair and blue eyes–by Iranian standards of course, which is not exactly Nordic. (My mother used to tell me, don't think you're pretty, you're just different.) My best friend in kindergarten, Niloofar, tells me that she used to go home after school and tell her mother that I was *rangi*–"colorful." She herself had the shiniest black hair, next only to my brother's, and silky skin the color of olive and bronze. She still has the same color scheme but my hair has not been blond in a long time. (There's an Iranian blonde for you.) The sun over there darkens the hair over time, unlike Californian sun that tends to bleach blond hair. Another "blonde" I used to know was Mitra in high school. Now, she had no business being blond at all. My mother's family were emigrants from the Caucasus after all, but she was Zoroastrian. Zoroastrians are mostly from Yazd and Kerman, and, believe me, very dark. Mitra had dark eyes, olive complexion, and her hair, underneath the outermost layer which was a rich golden blond, was darker back then than mine is now. I wonder what happened to her hair? (My hair was also straighter back then, but that's beside the point.)

We used to spend practically all our summers at the Caspian Sea. Our stretch of the coast was not what it is today, but I won't talk about how it's been ruined–I will only stick to good things. Before we had orange and apple and plum groves there used to be nothing but sand, save for where here and there some tall straw-like weeds grew. There is a picture of me when I'm about six years old holding a fish that some fisherman had just caught, and in the background where later there would be *qa-treh-tala* plum trees framed by rows of zinnias, there is nothing but sand. I have distinct recollection of trucks hauling good black forest soil from the other side of the road, dumping them on our property. I also have a vivid picture of Mash Qasem in my mind, pulling down a lever on a little machine, churning out cinder blocks from the mixture of cement with our very own sand. I remember the rows of blocks drying in the sun. It could not have been too long after that that our first *sakku* platform was built, the one closest to the sea. (Now with the change in the coast line much of all of this is completely under water.) In the earliest days we slept in a tent pitched on this sakku. Later a bigger sakku was built about half way between the road-gate and the sea-gate, and when walls went up and roof and doors and windows were installed, we had a summer house built on and of sand. The house was L-shaped and the shorter wing of the L was the children's sleeping quarter. When Afshin and his family vacationed with us he and I and our two brothers slept side by side on the wooden beds that our parents joined together to make room.

Our brothers were older and played together. They borrowed Mash Qasem's wheelbarrow and shovel to build dams on the beach, or took turns riding his huge bicycle on the newly-paved road running north of the property. I remember being a little afraid for them as I watched them trying to control the wobbling of the rusty front wheel. Afshin and I played together, year after year. That last summer we were still playing with plastic buckets and a gardening spade, and our sand constructions were quite crude compared to those of our brothers'. Actually, I wasn't the one making things at all; I was the gopher and the cheerleader. It was Afshin who did the building, and his favorite creation was a Mount Damavand that he patiently patted into a perfectly smooth cone, while I collected twigs and pebbles to landscape the base. We tried making streams and waterfalls for which I hauled water, passing the bucket from hand to hand and stretching out my other arm for balance. But no matter how well we paved the path of our streams with perfectly flat pebbles water seeped right through to the sand and vanished in a blink. We eventually gave up on the streams, but only after we had spent many an afternoon, right after lunch when the adults took naps and we were not allowed to swim, combing the beach, searching for wide and perfectly flat stones. I loved collecting stones. We found that they were prettier when wet–they had wavy patterns on them in subtle blue-green-gray colors– so we licked each one and watched it reveal its pattern and color. This fascination with stones led to our little stone factory where we pounded pebbles into powder, then tasted the powder. Stone powder is the smoothest and grittiest substance you can imagine, very fine until you put a pinch of it on your tongue.

Early afternoons were my favorite time of day. The sea is usually very calm then. It is green and calm, more enticing to children than the silver and calm of early evening which was when grownups liked to go swimming. (Mornings and late afternoons the sea was blue and a bit choppy.) Sometimes in the early afternoons Afshin and I hit the tomato and cucumber patches, salt-shaker in hand. The vegetables were warm from the sun and the cucumbers so tender they instantly sweated at the break when we snapped them. As we sat in the *jaliz* talking I would pull my dress down over my ankles but Afshin's bare legs were always being attacked by little stinging bugs. Once, while scratching the insect bites on his legs, he told me about his father climbing Mount Damavand and his promise to take him to the first base one of these times.

Some afternoons we went to Mash Qasem's house to sit with his wife on their sakku, the one closest to the road. While her husband and baby napped we found Fatemeh sitting on a faded gilim drinking her tea in quiet. That was her tea time; when people woke from their naps—her family and ours—she would be busy serving the tea. We sat cross-legged on her gilim and sometimes she would have a bowl of cherries for us. We would aim the cherry pits at her flock of chickens hovering around us. They dodged the cherry-pit bullets with the most ridiculous noise and flapping of wings and we would laugh, swallowing our breaths and covering our mouths in gestural recognition of the sleeping family.

One afternoon our last summer together, returning to the beach after fetching something, I saw Afshin in the distance kicking at something with such force that it made him spin around. As I got closer I saw how angry he was. I also suddenly noticed that he was much taller than he used to be.

Next time I saw Afshin it was later in the summer in Tehran at the house of a mutual friend. While sitting politely in the living room he told me that he and his brother were being sent off to boarding school in England. I hated England. I had read Hamlet in fourth grade and thought England was where people murdered each other by pouring poison down each other's ears. My hatred of England suddenly extended to the room where we were sitting. I wanted to kick the basket of fruit and the bowl of nuts off the coffee table. I wanted to throw the little bronze sculpture at my elbow through the window... Then we went outside, circling the swimming pool. The family had small children and metal railing around their pool. Afshin held on to the railing with one hand, pulling against it with the full weight of his body. He walked at an angle, and following his steps I did exactly as he did. He told me that he dreamt that Mount Damavand had a volcanic eruption. His hair was cut shorter than usual and my eyes were fixed on his hairline where there still was a trace of peeling sun-burnt skin.

Dobeyti: *Since from my dear Astrea's sight*
           I was so rudely torn
           My soul has never known delight
           Unless it were to mourn

When I was in high school my brother and my best friends all were sent abroad: my brother went to Switzerland; Marjan and Mehrdad went to England; and Fariba and her entire family moved to the U.S. I was in tenth grade when all this happened, and my most vivid memory of that year was that I read *The Red and the Black*. In fact, I read it many times consecutively, referring the whole time back and forth to the translator's Introduction which was a sort of critical essay. (I remember how hungry I felt for metatextual commentary, but this is also beside the point.) At the end of the school year I had four *tajdidis*–courses I had not passed and for which I had to retake examinations at the end of the summer. This was quite out of the ordinary for me, and my mother was alarmed. She sat me down one day and asked if I missed my brother and my friends and wanted to be sent to school in Europe too. (The U.S. was out of the question at that age.)

The offer had its titillating side: those color pictures my friends sent of photogenic foreign cities sprinkled with freedom and rock concerts... But then I thought of boarding school. Swiss boarding schools were too decadent in my view; I had seen my fresh-faced little friend, Afsaneh, come back wearing lipstick and smoking cigarettes. I did not like that. My brother had already decided he didn't like Switzerland and was about to leave to live with our uncle's family in the U.S. And when I thought about England I pictured the "guardians" I would be assigned, those flabby, white-faced characters who put a limp arm around you when *mamma* and *papa* took your picture with them before leaving you in their care. "Care"–good riddance. I figured if anybody was going to tell me what I could and could not do it might as well be my parents. Anyway, I could only think of Lowood when I thought of British boarding schools; that's where Jane Eyre was sent. And me, well, I was thinking a lot more about Mathilde de la Mole than Jane Eyre. So I said no thank you to my mother and decided to stay in Iran. She was happy about it and I to this day am too–especially when years later I heard about the racism (what was that?) my friends encountered in British boarding schools. And the niggardliness. A boarding school victim friend told me a while ago that it took her a long time before she found white friends, and that each week they were only given fresh top sheets for their beds; the bottom ones were to be replaced by the already-used top sheets. Why would anyone subject themselves to that if they had any say in it?

So come fall I happily went back to my all-girl high school, the old Nourbakhsh high school, the new Reza Shah Kabir. My school had the reputation of being a "bad-girl" high school. The girls were considered tough, fast and free. (Free, that is, "up to a point," as Mr. Brooke says in *Middlemarch*, "up to a point.") Anyway, I never had tajdidis again, and six months after graduating from highs chool I turned eighteen and was shipped off to college in the U.S.

My friend Jean-Jacques's father had been a POW in Germany. As a Belgian he had no good experience of Germans at all, and yet when Jean-Jacques was growing up he was sent to Germany to live with the people and learn the language. Jean-Jacques's father sent his son to the *other* side, and I admired him for two reasons. One was that he bore no hatred, and two, that he recognized who the "other" was. That menacing Other, the one who is your enemy, is practically of your own flesh and blood; it's your next door neighbor. It is not somebody half way around the world, about whom you know nothing. To my eyes, coming from half way around the world, Europe seemed so homogeneous that the variety of hatred appeared as varieties of self-contempt. And Jean-Jacques, I think, still roams around the world looking for an out of a local brutality. I never heard him use the word exotic but he seemed only interested in nonwhite women: Latin American black and brown, Middle Eastern, East Asian, Indian. Now I wonder if he just always wanted to go somewhere far away: *gate, gate, paragate, parasamgate...* (Some of us just must.) Exotic is the limit of our own imagination. Anyway, this is not about Jean-Jacques, it's about someone else.

It's about Arash. His father is Iranian and his mother English. He called a while ago to say that he had gotten married. A few weeks later I got a letter from him where he informed me that he had "extinguished cravings" and his "romantic and nostalgic yearnings have been declared redundant." ("Oh no," I thought, "stiff and clammy as a peeled raw potato.") It was he who said of his American wife (she's blond, I saw her picture): She's not exotic like Iranian girls. And I would not be writing this if a couple of years ago it had not come to me in a dream (it really did) that he and I belonged together. I never mentioned my dream, but "kindred spirits" were his words. I would add that we were sister and brother of sorts.

My mother may not be British but my godmothers are: English women writers are the godmothers of most present-day writing women. There is such a thing as genealogy and perhaps women writers all over the world owe a debt of anxious influence (as they say) to, really, inevitably, certain great pillars of thinking womanhood: Mary Wollstonecraft, Jane Austen, Mary Shelley, the Brontës, George Eliot, Virginia Woolf, Doris Lessing, Angela Carter... As for our fathers, Arash himself being, literally, the son of a Fereydoun, I always felt a bit shy to say that I too claimed descent from Fereydoun: the legitimate shah whose mother fled with him as an infant to India so he would be raised in safety on milk from a sacred cow, and whose education she later entrusted to a wise hermit in the Alborz range in Iran. It was Fereydoun who was to liberate us from that primeval and primordial tyrant, the patricide Zahhak, who fed the brains of young men to the snakes that grew from his shoulders. The snakes' appetite brought devastation to

Iranian people and Zahhak's fearful search for his nem-
esis Fereydoun brought ruin to even the animals of the
kingdom. Alas, I fantasized a good deal about that ho-
liest alliance between Kaveh the iron-smith who led a
rebellion against Zahhak after losing one too many sons,
and Fereydoun the noble and the free. Perhaps I suffered
from a Cordelia complex.

But if to Jean-Jacques the future seemed to be
hidden in a far-away place, to Arash that far away place
was his past. You see, he was sent to boarding school in
England when he was not yet ten years old. His Persian was not very good and I can only imagine how bad
he must have felt not being able to decipher his father's
shekasteh handwriting in his letters. I think this has always
been more hurtful to Arash than he admits. So much
so that if you tell him the story of Fereydoun dividing
his realm between his three sons—Salm, Tour and Iraj—
he takes it as if you're threatening him with existential
extinction. He will push you off your own delicate balance on the precipice, or run from you, when he finds
you know the story of Salm, the prince of wealth who
inherited Rum, Tur, the prince of valor, who inherited
Touran, and Iraj, the prince of order and justice, who
inherited Iran—Iran, the land of *gem-strewn borders*, where
art was revealed superior to riches... This sort of thing, Vita
Nuova to me, is a nostalgic black hole to Arash, a spell,
a beckoning without the illumination of language and
story. What did he really think about being named after
Arash, the aged hero, the greatest archer in the land, who
with the last of his life force released the arrow that would
define the border of Iran with Touran? I understand it
is not fair. I mean, why would a Fereydoun name his son
Arash and send him to boarding school in England? It is

confounding. But if you don't look irony in the face you are doomed to pursue each other to the North Pole like Victor Frankenstein and his creation did. Arash is thus divided, a romantic division that he rightly diagnosed as connected to nostalgia.

Sometimes I feel like a fat and jolly bodhisattva, sitting here with my ears long-lobed like the floppy ears of the motherless elephant who was the incarnation of Lord Buddha. *I am like the center of a circle, equidistant from all points on the circumference.* Sometimes I glimpse a pair of eyes looking at me from the circumference, expectant, as it were. Yes, yes, yes, I see, I'd like to say. I laugh. It should be one thing but it's definitely another. Or, as that other poet put it: *It is impossible to say just what I mean.*

Let me try again... I feel I am as exotic and as much as an English writer as Arash is English and the son of a Fereydoun, and we are both floating on the circumference of a circle. Perhaps irony is the tension between opposite points on this circle. Perhaps the circle itself is the circle of paradox. Who knows. What I would like to say is that I don't, over all, consider it my business to point out ironies. That sort of thing is on the periphery. What I tried to say to Arash, though it's impossible to say just what one means, is that what really matters is the lyric. That's what lies in the center.

By way of introduction Arash said of his American wife, "she's no poet." I have no interest in speculating about what goes into people's connection to each other. Who knows what cravings must be extinguished in favor of which. Who knows what serves as a muse for whom. What's in it for me is the realization that there is such a thing as having no use for a muse—or a poet. But I didn't say anything about this. Let there be silence, I decided. But I was wrong. I should have told him to go fuck himself.

At any rate, it is not the muse who giveth and it is not the muse who taketh away. It is the poet.

Dobeyti: *But, oh, alas, with weeping eyes*
                  And bleeding heart I lie
                  Thinking on her whose absence 'tis
                  That makes me wish to die

Two Thousand Five Hundred Years

Exactly one year after the celebrations of the 2,500th anniversary of the founding of the Persian Empire, the film *Foroughe Javedan,* Eternal Glory, was released. It was to commemorate a celebration that people were trying to forget as an embarrassing spectacle. And as far as anybody knew, bused school children were the only audience for the film. On a clear and crisp fall morning in 1973 it was the turn of the students of Reza Shah Kabir high school in Tehran to go see it.

The girls were accustomed to school-sponsored excursions. School children were early on introduced to putting in appearances before the Shah's family or visiting heads of state. They were taken to line up the streets and clap when waving royalty passed by in their convertibles, usually to or from the airport. Mitra remembered applauding the motorcades of Haile Selassi of Ethiopia, Mobuto Sese Seco of Zaire, King Hossein of Jordan, and any number of less memorable dignitaries. The days typically started out fun for the kids but slowly dissipated into the boredom of endless waiting around. A quick glimpse of some benevolently smiling western leader with a coiffed lady by his side, or some exotically dressed character from Africa or Asia, was hardly enough compensation for sore feet or a minor heat stroke.

But the practice did familiarize children with the names of some foreign countries and their leaders. The kids formed likes and dislikes. Sometimes they even became attached to foreign leaders they hadn't even had the opportunity to applaud. JFK was one. When he was assassinated a ditty made the rounds of Tehran preschools:

> *God, why can't it be for Kennedy to come back to life?*
> *Kennedy was kind, he was a friend to children*

More than just a few little kids found the Kennedy assassination so sad as to have a good cry over their projects at the handicrafts table.

But as security became tighter, the bonding ritual between world leaders and Iranian school children was abandoned. By the 1970s the days of spotting royalty and their cohorts in convertibles were long over.

On the day of the Eternal Glory viewing, Reza Shah Kabir girls walked en masse to Cinema Royal. The theater was walking distance from their school but the plan to walk there may not have been a wise one. Seven or eight hundred high schoolgirls descending on the streets was virtually unsupervisable. And not any high school either... Reza Shah Kabir High School had quite a reputation for its unruly girls. You see, Reza Shah Kabir was the new name for the old Noorbakhsh High School, sister to Alborz High School for boys, founded by Presbyterian Americans. The progressive missionaries had provided an introduction to American-style democracy, and freedom from the traditional Iranian autocratic and punitive approach to education. A kind of free spirit prevailed in these schools and even after they fell under Iranian management they still retained a bit of their devil-may-care culture and certainly their reputation for fostering an almost arrogant independence in their students.

The day of the movie excursion the girls were in crisp uniforms and in top form. When alone, girls were vulnerable on Tehran streets, zigzagging their way through male foot traffic with downcast eyes. They clutched their books to their chests, dodging groping hands and obscene comments. But together they were bold. Such a big group was unstoppable.

As the procession walked on, the more aggressive girls in the front rows linked arms and charged men off the sidewalks and into the car traffic. No poor street vendor was spared. The little kiosks selling cigarettes, newspapers, and lottery tickets were the easiest targets.

"Mister, may I have a cigarette… please?" a girl batting her eyelashes went up to a kiosk.

"All right, just one…," the vendor jovially pulled out a pack. A pretty girl tapping his chest with a manicured finger was not something that happened to him every day.

"But what about me…?" another girl snatched the pack.

"And me?"

Before he knew what was happening, the vendor and his pack of cigarettes were pounced on by half a dozen girls. Then the girls threw the empty pack over their shoulders and laughed in the poor man's face.

"You sluts. You whores. I'll fuck your mothers…," the vendor yelled after them, extra frustrated because he was unable to abandon his kiosk to chase them.

Meanwhile the next batch of girls arrived on the scene. "Don't scream so hard mister," said a saucy one. "Your milk will dry up."

Other vendors clamored to get out of the way as they saw the girls approaching. The medium bold girls egged on the boldest and the timid ones huddled together, laughing little mousy laughs. When school officials were not looking, the radical contingent of the girls—the ones who exchanged newspapers clippings with pictures of Leyla Khaled, Bernadette Devlin, and Angela Davis—flashed V signs to the cars stopped behind red lights and occasionally got a V sign back.

When they arrived at Cinema Royal the girls were worked up and ready to assert their collective presence. The build-up, however, had been even longer in the making.

A year before, during the celebrations themselves, all schools were closed for a week, ostensibly for children to "participate" in the festivities. A week of holidays was of course always welcome for students but the national mood was far from festive. To begin with, apart from official receptions for arriving foreign dignitaries there *were* no festivities. The city was under a kind of siege. Rumors flew about. There was talk of martial law being declared for the entire city. There was talk of the secret police taking inventory of inhabitants of certain neighborhoods and placing all their communication under surveillance. Who knew the truth, but the rank and file police officers who normally had nothing to show for their authority but their blue caps and a dangling baton now carried guns. In the months leading to the celebrations there had been many demonstrations at the universities. News spread by word of mouth while the media was silent.

But no matter; on this day the girls were irrepressible. The pomp and circumstance of the celebrations, far from inspiring awe and pride, was a made-to-order pretext for the display of irreverence. And the darkness of the movie theater was a dream cover. Hooting and hollering accompanied the scenes of royal receptions. The coterie of the Shah's fellow third world strongmen—Suharto, Marcos, Yahya Khan, etc.—brought out loud jeering. The stony-faced Eastern bloc delegations and their beefy wives drew grunts from the teenaged girls.

"Teacher, may I…?" one voice feigning earnestness was raised when President Giri of India made his appearance. "Do Indian leaders always have to be on the verge of starvation?"

The most popular celebrity was Constantine of Greece, all dapper and freshly deposed, whom the girls greeted with applause and whistles and chants of "Eddy, Eddy…"—for Eddy Constantine. Some tried to take up similar cheering for handsome Juan Carlos of Spain but were shouted down with a rebuff from a few ironic voices: "Franco, Franco…" The idea was to remind everyone that Franco had put Juan Carlos on the throne.

Haile Selassie, Emperor of Ethiopia and the Lion of Judah, touted as the highest ranking guest, was reported to have traveled with an entourage of 72 and a poodle with a diamond-studded collar. He was always at the Shah's side during the ceremonies and absorbed the ridicule that not even in the darkness of the theater did the girls dare to hurl at the Shah himself.

The official opening of the celebrations was the speech delivered by the Shah before the tomb of Cyrus the Great. The site for this ceremony was Pasargad, the buried city neighboring Persepolis. The tomb of Kourosh (Persian for Cyrus), an unassuming structure, had stood in a neglected mausoleum for millenia. For these ceremonies, however, the area was cleared of ancient debris (what's a little history to a photo op?), turned into a flat stage where elegant bleachers were set up and colorful umbrellas protected the dignitaries from the unrelenting sun of the region. A vast blue platform streaked with gleaming red carpets was laid before the modest tomb of Kourosh. The crimson stripes down the side of the gilded black pants of the Shah and his generals and cabinet ministers echoed the red carpet. And the queen in her white silk gown trimmed with green and gold brocade cut a regal figure. Only the unsightly criss-crossing black cords of the recording and amplifying equipment were a visual blight. The event was photographed, among others, by the personal photographer of the Kennedy family.

When the Shah walked up to the tomb there was a hint of a hush among the girls in the movie theater. It was as if they were reassessing the spectacle one last time. But by the time the Shah began delivering the famous lines of his speech that had become the butt of endless jokes, the girls had recovered themselves.

"*Kourosh...*," enunciated the Shah into a multitude of microphones.

"*Jooooon...?*" the girls screeched with hilarity.

"*King of kings...*"

"We're listening, *jigar...*"

"S*leep in peace for we are awake.*"

"So are we, SO ARE WE...!" the girls shrieked in unison and all hell broke loose in the theater. They were beside themselves. The wild cheering, whistling, and stamping of feet drowned the rest of the Shah's speech.

That was the moment everyone had been waiting for.

One of the highlights of the celebrations was the parade of soldiers from different dynastic eras. The parade was accompanied by earsplitting original marches commissioned for period instruments. Leading the procession were Achamenid soldiers in outfits familiar to everyone from Persepolis bas-reliefs. The girls covered their ears and laughed out loud at the goofy costumes and sloppy marching.

The gentlemen attired as ancient soldiers were instructed not to shave for months and had acquired massive round beards that grew almost right up to their eyes. With their short foreheads they barely showed any skin, and putting on the required stern expressions they looked quite menacing (little could anyone guess that in a few short years the look would make a come-back in Islamic garb). Down the line from the copiously bearded ancients were the Safavid soldiers with shaved chins, sporting mustaches that extended beyond their cheeks. Finally, the modern soldiers arrived in crisp uniforms with white spats on their shoes and faces shaved smooth and shiny.

"The history of Gillette," a girl loudly declared at the end of the *défiler*.

A couple of teachers joined in the laughter.

But the movie droned on and on and the girls lost interest. The show was just not up to the level of audience spirit. Some of the older girls started sneaking out to meet up with boyfriends they had called from phone booths on the way to the theater. Others to whom ditching school was not an option broke into groups discussing various subjects among themselves. The first thing that was scrutinized was the fashion sense of the dignitaries.

The consensus was that their own queen was the best dressed.

"I like the silk outfits they make for her with traditional batik motifs."

"But the hats are ridiculous. Why does she wear them?"

"She can't have her hair done all the time."

"No, it's a royalty thing. Haven't you seen the queen of England? They have to wear hats. It makes them stand out."

"The queen of Denmark doesn't wear hats. And she's the most dignified."

"Imelda Marcos doesn't either and she is so vulgar."

"She wishes some of our queen's dignity would rub off on her. You could just see it when Farah was picking her up at the airport and they were standing side by side listening to the national anthem. Imelda Marcos kept throwing side glances at Farah."

"What boring stuff these royalty have to do. Farah looks bored a lot."

"She's stiff. That's her idea of acting like royalty."

"No. My mother says she looks mad at the Shah. She says she's miserable. The Shah cheats on her."

"She probably goes shopping when she's mad. She has so many clothes."

"And so much jewelry. These things that the royals plunk on their heads and pin to their chests are so huge they're ugly."

A pained expression came over the face of one of the shy girls. "There's something ugly about jewels," she said. "I mean, the things these people do so they get to wear these stupid things and do these stupid things…"

she motioned to the screen, then blushed at her own in-articulate exertion.

"The communists, they don't wear jewelry," someone continued.

That reminded them of the evening gowns of the eastern bloc ladies.

"I guess fashion is not socialist," said one girl. "Their gowns are so frumpy. I wonder if Madame Tito and Madame Padgorny are jealous of these western la-dies…"

Then the conversation turned to male royalty and their ornaments.

"I don't understand this medal business," said someone. "I thought you had to earn medals. These guys give themselves medals."

"I think European royalty inherit medals. But we don't have that tradition. Where did the Shah's medals come from?"

"At least the Shah doesn't wear the kind that dan-gle from a chain."

"Yes he does. Such heavy gold chains too… Pari Zanjiri could put them to good use."

Pari Zanjiri was a Reza Shah Kabir High School legend. She had taken off her heavy antique necklace—one of those that were made popular by the sixties' fash-ion discovery of ethnic jewelry—and swung it above her head during a fight at a volleyball game with her school's arch rival, Azar High School. She had certainly done her opponents some damage that day.

"Malek Hossein wears those too, the little jerk…"

A short discussion about which of the world lead-ers looked most like jerks followed. Someone nominated the Persian Gulf sheikhs. Others said at least they had some authenticity, not copying European royalty in their attire.

"They say they had to get them raw camel meat at the banquets," one of the girls made a face. "They don't eat all that French stuff, you know…"

"Raw…?" The girls laughed. "But those stuffed peacocks on the tables–did they actually eat them?"

No one knew. They returned to the jerk competition, which ended with a tie between King Hossein and Marcos.

"Which of the world leaders look most like butchers?" someone whispered conspiratorially.

"Suharto."

"Ceauşescu."

"No, Suharto. Suharto."

A certain bad-taste-in-the-mouth that the girls were trying to avoid all day was becoming pronounced. The ousting of Sukarno reminded Iranians of the coup against Mosaddeq, and the girls' jeering mood stopped right there. They fell silent and turned to the movie again.

It was now showing the rejoicing of the populace. Picture perfect village scenes were staged for the benefit of foreign guests and journalists. Happy villagers, colorful costumes, dancing, stomping, chanting… What might not have struck foreign observers, however, were little things like, oh, those women with their magnificent layered skirts were tribal nomads and did not belong to these villages, or the outfits worn by the men actually belonged to people from a different part of the country. Surely the foreigners noticed the manicured fingers of some of the ladies in tribal attire? No matter. It was a rare city kid who did not know what village life really was like. Relatives, neighbors, servants, weekend hikes, and any travel from anywhere to anywhere brought them close to it. Creased faces, ragged clothes, hungry children smelling like goats, hardened whey balls strewn with livestock hair... Who hadn't noticed that to a village child a fitting pair of shoes was a dream, that women lost their teeth and looked fifty at twenty five, and children dropped dead from dysentery? Who hadn't seen the malnourished babies with bloated stomachs and large heads flattened in the back from being strapped to their cribs all day?

Then again, who hadn't played in the orchards in the villages, picked fragrant fruit that had to be checked for worms, hiked in the hills with the dizzying smell of herbs and wild flowers, eaten fried eggs with bright orange yokes and *vaalak* rice with green garlic? Who hadn't drunk from the ice-cold springs that bubbled from dark holes on the side of mountains and stepped on wobbly rocks crossing gushing rivers? Who hadn't felt the pulse of the dusty earth under their feet–bare or clad in good shoes–village and city folk alike?

Eternal glory had dissipated into an eternal yawn for the girls.

"*Basseh digeh*," someone suddenly blurted out in the quieted-down theater. "Enough already." The film had gone on far too long and, actually, the celebrations themselves had become an irrelevant blip in the cares and concerns of the nation. What nonsense. What waste. Whatever.

Even Reza Shah girls lost their exuberance by the end of the movie that disappeared forever in some un-indexed archive. Unlike the morning, however, the girls' walk back to school was dispersed and subdued.

EXOTICA

I must go back briefly to a place I have loved
to tell you those you will efface I have loved.
                                        Agha Shahid Ali

The Color Black

It is the 1980s in Iran. The country is pervaded with the color black.

This is not the solitary and sorrowful black we are accustomed to see worn in mourning for forty days or a year. Nor is it the dramatic black of the banners of the *Tasu'a* and *Ashura* mourning processions, flying against a backdrop of white cotton and green silk, bringing to life the massacre of the Seventy Two Innocents and drawing tears from the great Lion of Persia. This is a new color. It can be the color of lead—opaque and massive—as in the paint on the windows of the whitewashed building of Chalus Hotel turned interrogation center and prison.

Small towns in the Mazandaran province on the Caspian coast, Chalus and its neighboring Nowshahr, were favored by the Shah and his father as summer resorts. Before the revolution these towns prospered on account of waves of summer tourists from Tehran. They became associated with decadence: nightclubs, luxurious private villas, bare female skin on the beaches. Now that the villas are for the most part abandoned by their mostly exiled owners, and women are allowed to bathe only in carefully secluded and patrolled areas in pants, overgarments, and head scarves, these towns are nevertheless subjected to an above average degree of Islamic surveillance.

On any hot and humid morning, a rusty Peykan of Nowshahr police with its makeshift Allah emblem, paces the streets warning the population, through an ancient bullhorn, of the punitive consequences of *badhejabi* (being ill-veiled) and other social offenses. The offwhite Nissan Patrol of the Revolutionary Guards, the fearful Pasdars, with its fleet of a Peykanful of black-veiled Sisters in tow, circles the streets in silence. In Chalus, the windows of the charming colonial building of Hotel Chalus are painted over with black paint while passersby walk and drive by it in feigned oblivion lest they arouse the suspicion of the Pasdars lining the roof and porches of the building.

Or the black can be glossy and piercing, as in the glance of revolutionary guards following one's movements as one walks by. It cuts through our animated conversation one day as I descend the stairs of an apartment building into the street with my friends. I am in company of three men to whom I am unrelated—an offense punishable for all of us by, at least, flogging—when we unexpectedly come face to face with a sight we must ignore and leave behind as quickly as we can. A man, still behind the steering wheel of his car and deathly pale in the face, answers the questions of the Pasdars hovering over him. His car is cornered by three Nissan Patrols against which some of the guards lean, pointing their G3 semi-automatics in our direction and following our steps with their eyes. We lower our voice but do not altogether stop, and walk briskly but casually to our car. One more time we escape being the immediate subject of their attention.

Black is the color of fear. Strapped to the *ta'zir* platform, J, picked up in a phone booth in a situation of being in the wrong place at the wrong time, or simply because of "suspicious appearance," is flogged for information at *Sho'beh* 5 of Evin Prison. She is beaten on the bottoms of her feet with wire cables. No exotic method of torture, this most common form of ta'zir has proved to serve the purpose well. J is left alone when her feet become numb, only for the ta'zir session to be resumed when the wounds have "cooled off"—which in Evin parlance means the feet and legs have swollen and the nerves have become active again. She is periodically left alone with pen and paper to write her confessions. She is confronted with other prisoners who might recognize her, or she them, before being transferred to a room where detainees—bleeding, delirious with pain, or temporarily insane—are kept between interrogation sessions.

Strapped down, intermittently conscious, J lives the timelessness of pain. She remembers nothing, she knows nothing, but pain. Sometimes she is left for minutes, sometimes for hours. Unable to anticipate the next ta'zir session, the boundaries of pain and fear of pain give, and she succumbs to the permanence of the moment. She falls asleep when she is left alone to write. She even falls asleep under the lashes, frustrating and provoking her interrogators more. In the communal room she grabs hold of the skirt of a woman who stands up with a jolt in the middle of the night shaking her head and muttering to herself, pulls her down to the floor, and they both sleep.

Blindfolded as you are, you see nothing but black. Tied down to the board with your head covered by a folded blanket, you breathe black. And in the omnipresent sound of *noheh* chants echoing in the interrogation chambers of *Komiteh Markazi*—as a woman is lashed in the presence of her crying little boy—you hear a harrowing, ironic black: *Aseman khun geryeh kon farzande Zahra mizanand*—Shed tears of blood, sky, the child of Zahra is beaten.

It was one morning at work when Z received a call from her husband in Evin. His case had finally gone to trial and, two years after his arrest, his death sentence was issued. He had called to hear her voice, but thinking of sparing her one last night he had not told her of the sentence. Nevertheless she had sensed death and had broken down at the office. Dragging her two-year-old daughter to Evin the next day, in the irrational hope that they might take pity on the child, she was informed that the sentence had been carried out at dawn.

At that moment, she said, she detested all hope: her own and his. Not that she was afraid—she had spent her years at Evin too. Under extreme physical pain she had learned how what is temporary can be eternal and how even this eternity shall pass. Enduring the pain but remaining unyielding, her belief was tested and confirmed: the future, change, freedom will triumph. But that morning when she suddenly saw her husband devoured by the beast of the struggle for freedom, everything in her mind vanished but one word: Hamid. Through the days that followed, she felt the sound of his name pounding unrelentingly inside her head, claiming, as it were, the man inside the sacrificial dress.

In prison, she had come to know the power to wipe out any existence, temporary or eternal. She had learned to stop the most automatic train of thought. She had stopped herself from thinking about her injuries, wiping off her mind the image of the lacerated flesh on her feet and legs. Through the long feverish days of her infected wounds, she had denied pain, thinking of cool water, of waves and rivers. But now "Hamid" pounded in her ears. The existence of this pain she was incapable of obliterating. She felt the swelling of a hard, massive rage—a black stone germinating from deep earth—pressing against her every fiber. And in a secretly held memorial service for her husband, she sat, unmoved, through the bitter words of a friend's eulogy: "The blood shed for liberty and for Islam have mixed and dissolved in one another underneath the ground of the fields of poppy and tulip. That which grows on this blood over time, let us call it *progress*. So shall progress, too, become a legacy of the Islamic Republic."

Black Blood (what have you done)

When my cousin Firouzeh disappeared from a phone booth on Takhte Tavoos Avenue my mother and uncle were still in Iran. My aunt, Firouzeh's mother, had help from her sister and brother looking for Firouzeh. In the year after they located her in Evin, my mother escaped though Turkey and my uncle smuggled his draft-age boys out of the country. My aunt was left alone, caring for their mother and visiting Firouzeh at Evin. Luckily my grandmother lived to see Firouzeh's release, but died before I went to Tehran. In her last pictures she had a wide-eyed look with terror in her eyes.

My other grandmother's sister was still alive when I visited next summer and after having suffered a stroke and losing her speech she had the same wild look in her eyes. She sat wringing her hands and repeating the only thing she could say: "Dadeh shodeh." It was a meaningless phrase but we knew what she meant. She was referring to that dark cloud that rained pain and agony on us. I will never forget that unsheltered feeling of huddling together under black rain, giving each other pitiful smiles of courage.

Firouzeh suffered from bad headaches after Evin. I tried to give her relaxing massages. I would put my hands on her skinny back, running my fingers over the two tight ropes stretching from the base of her skull down to her pelvis. I felt her clenched upper trapezius muscles. I traced the ta'zir scars on her feet, where she had been flogged for information. I tried to release the toes that were slightly clawed by the pull of scar tissue. I didn't so much massage her as stroke her. Lying on her back, I supported the weight of her head and upper back in my hands and just ran my fingers over the tangled soft tissue.

I had a kinesiology teacher who used to say that the study of fascia to the body is what geology is to the earth. Fascia is the connective tissue that keeps every part of the body separate yet connected. It is layers of body memory. Like a blind person whose fingertips read the Braille of the body, I absorbed something of these memories. My fingertips picked up things that neither Firouzeh nor I could put into words. Friends who had nursed her infected feet, with whom she had huddled under the black rain in Evin, were still jailed. When I looked at my own hands they seemed stained black.

The day Firouzeh was released in Iran was night time where I was staying with my friend Fariba on the East Coast. My mother called me from California as soon as she heard the news and by the time the phone was passed on to me Fariba's entire household had been woken up. It was good news for a change. And I was so happy that I felt like falling at Khomeini's feet, kissing his hands and thanking him. Pure gratitude.

Firouzeh is a superb artist. She has always been an excellent painter but when a few years ago she took up sculpture it was as if she had done that all her life. My favorite works of hers, however, are two old paintings that she has left unfinished. They are pictures of women in black veils, twisted in mourning over half-dug graves. A strange yellow light emanates from the upturned earth.

What have you done?

The Party

It is still the 1980s in Iran. The famous translator SK and his wife are at the party. It is late in the evening and as the last of the host's supply of homemade *araq* is relentlessly attacked we listen to SK's tribulations in his most recent project: translating T.S. Eliot for publication in an unforeseeable future.

He suddenly turns to me. "And what is it that you—daughter of a translator, come from America—want to do?"

I say that I want to write. "I grew up on translation and have been living in translation since I left Iran. I'm tired of translations."

He asks what I am working on, and I explain that I hope to make an article out of the notes I have been taking on my trip.

"If you want to communicate with English speakers you have to use the language they understand, right?" he asks.

I agree.

"I will help you," he says. "Try this on Iran," and he quotes in English from T.S. Eliot:

> *The eyes are not here*
> *There are no eyes here*
> *In this valley of dying stars*
> *In this hollow valley*
> *This broken jaw of our lost kingdoms*

He pauses to take a sip of his drink. Then he asks, "Will you write about someone like me?"

I say that perhaps I should.

"Then write that this is my message—the message of a drunk old Iranian translator, clawing, to the best of his ability, the insides of the belly of the beast"— and he quotes from Eliot again:

> *Not for me the martyrdom, the ecstasy of thought and*
> *   prayer,*
> *Not for me the ultimate vision.*

As the sour-cherry Vishnovka is brought in, he pours himself another drink. "Go forth, daughter, and translate," his son mocks him. SK tastes the Vishnovka with concentration, compliments the hostess on the liqueur's perfect degree of sweetness, ignores his son, and continues on a more sober note.

"Translation is a practice too humble for most

people. The work itself, when it is successful, becomes obsolete the moment it is read. The reader, having taken one step toward understanding something foreign is immediately ready for the next step—and this frustrates the sophisticated reader. In the west, he blames translation for coming between himself and the original work, and given the inevitability of this mediation he is likely to give up in a huff. He is impatient to go directly, somehow magically, to the heart of the matter—as Goethe thought he did with Hafez. Or, rarely, he may recognize a kindred wit and run with it—as Voltaire did with Sa'di.

"But for the most part the western reader does not, *will not*, accept the idea of translation. It is inconceivable to him that things—especially if they come from the east—can only become accessible in degrees. No, he wants all or nothing. It's quite imperialistic really... Add the fact that the east is only recognized when it is *exotic*— which means inaccessible and implicitly erotic—and we can guess at the violence that this inspires: take things by force, violate, rape... But then God forbid that our words ring familiar—then we surely must be *westernized*."

"Westernization...," someone barges in. "The only thing that really means is that we speak their language and they don't speak ours."

"I think there are two solutions to the problem— at least as far as the literary world is concerned," SK goes on. "First, do let us forget about *texts*. My generation of translators did not translate *texts*. In our innocence we merely translated life and death and all that comes in between—as expressed in foreign words. You may want to call it writing but this is what needs to be translated *from* our language now. Second—and forgive me for saying so myself—the translator must be reckoned with. We are neither native-informants nor proselytes of any sort. Readers, interpreters, mediators, *we* are the problems of translation."

Then he turns to me. "And you had better not get tired of translation so soon. You still have less choice than you think."

SK's wife has been fidgeting for a while. At her own house, once she has cleared the dinner table, she might be persuaded to bring out her notebook and read her own poetry. But now she has decided that her husband has had enough to drink and is worried about the alcohol on his breath if they are stopped at a Revolutionary Guard checkpoint on their way home.

"It is not necessary to give the situation such epic dimensions," she says by way of wrapping up the conversation. "I think there is an invisible little difference at work here. There is a fundamental incongruity in aesthetics... Forget about genuinely foreign things; western art likes to make even familiar things strange. This is no secret—it's all over their literary theory. And we are—Iranians are—just the opposite. We go to any length to make foreign things our own. We even name our sons after Alexander, Genghiz Khan, and Tamerlane—those most brutal conquerors of our country. For us nothing is sweeter than setting eyes on the familiar: *Bashad ke baz binim didar-e ashena ra.* This is how in our poetry the Great Unknown is beckoned near... but we must be going now."

The line is a famous one from Hafez: "Would it that we may set eyes on the familiar one again."

She, MM, perhaps one of the best Iranian poets writing at present, stopped publishing her work a while ago. SK recites her poetry and she edits his translations, but she refuses to publish. Earlier, as she pored over someone's new Robert Frost acquisition, I thought I saw a smile flicker across her face when she read the lines: *Love at the lips was touch/As sweet as I could bear...*

SK has his own interpretation.

"It is as if there is a sleep from which she doesn't want to be awakened." And then he can't help paraphrasing Eliot: "She fears that human voices will wake her and she will drown."

In preparation for leaving, MM disappears inside her Islamic garb and produces a few cardamom pods from her purse. I learn that cardamom seeds work well for camouflaging the smell of alcohol on the breath.

"Don't be deceived by her lyric spirit," says SK as he stumbles to the door, popping the seeds in his mouth. "She is so resourceful she would make an excellent double agent."

Later, lying in bed at dawn and watching the outline of the Alborz range emerge from the dark, I have the vision that we have collected our belongings and are sleepwalking out of our old family house when the dormant volcano, our majestic Mount Damavand, erupts. The explosion floods us with light as we freeze in midflight. Dazed and awakened in various degrees, we retrace our steps, set down our things, and settle down once more.

The Black Hole of Survival

The memoir of the founder of one of Iran's biggest publishing houses, Amir Kabir, finally came out in 2004. In his memoir Taqi Jafari uses an image that has stayed with me.

As he tells the story, a few years before the revolution many people sensed the impending crisis. "This crown prince of ours will never make it to the throne," he says they muttered under their breath. One of Jafari's associates advised him to cash in his assets and emigrate to the U.S. before it was too late. But Jafari would not dream of it. "I have nothing to fear from a change in the regime," he said. "I have served my country and these books are my roots. Who can cut off my roots?" But of course the change was ruinous to him. He describes it as the felling of a tree he had planted. "The tree was axed, the roots were severed, the branches and leaves wilted, and the bloom withered." Writing his memoirs he found himself not just recounting his life and work but contemplating the "hole left in the ground by the uprooted tree."

The reference to this hole makes the image of the uprooted tree doubly apt. One can picture the felled tree with its mighty roots and branches a testament to years of nurture and growth, the magnificent living thing whose life has been cut short. But the tree, in its mutilated form, is visible no matter how hard the regime tries to obstruct the view—what begs for closer inspection is the black hole left in the ground by the uprooting. This black hole has swallowed a great deal over the years.

What cultural revolutions try to do is not just chop down trees such as Jafari's, as monuments of the old order of things, but bury the past in the hole that is left behind. The analogy is not mine. After the revolution, the new regime called the publication of books by authors from pre-revolution days "exhumation." It did its best to bury the intelligentsia along with a certain past. Exploring the hole left by the uprooted tree exposes the falsifications that a cultural revolution is based on, but it turns up a great deal more.

This dark hole has swallowed four decades of life. Big chunks of the lives of roughly three generations have now vanished into it—from the peak years of the older generation to the childhood of the youngest. I belong to the middle generation whose coming of age coincided with the revolution. Many died in war and by execution. Many were crushed or lost years in prison. Many, many left Iran. But most of us who survived, inside or outside Iran, have found ourselves sliding into the black hole little by little, day by day.

My old elementary school principal, Touran Mirhhadi, a celebrated educator, wrote about struggles against death in her own memoir and the biography of her German mother who moved to Iran in the 1920s: first and second world wars, occupation of Iran, famine, disease, third-world backwardness—and struggles for social change. Those were heroic struggles. My generation's struggle against death has hardly amounted to more than our own daily survival, reeling from blows while trying to make it from one day to the next. So far we have lost the decades of our lives from, let's say, our twenties to sixties. While my generation was thrown off its life's path, the generations after us did not even have the luxury of envisioning such a path. Postponed life, aborted plans, decisions never made, despair, loss, waste—this is the stuff floating inside the darkness of the past four decades. Years went by as we strained to see the light at the end of the tunnel. This seemingly endless wait has been part of Iranian life, within or without the country's borders.

Marz, "border," is an interesting Persian word. It means both the outer limits of a physical space as well as the area enclosed within those limits. *Marz-e por gohar*—a phrase from *Ey Iran*, the country's national anthem by popular consensus—refers to Iran as a country of jewel-strewn *marz*. Iranians refer to themselves as either *doroun-marzi*, within borders, or *boroun-marzi*, outside borders. Studded with gems or not, *marz* becomes little more than an arbitrary designation to those alienated within or displaced without borders.

"Exile" does not only apply to Iranians living outside Iran; it is also the condition of being denied history and existence inside the country. Denial, in fact, is the first thrust in digging black holes. Perhaps the twentieth century will go down in history for the range and depth of its denials. The sheer number of its cultural revolutions, which were busier with the denial and eradication of the past than the building of future, would support this claim. Certainly a great deal of the best literature of the twentieth century, from Russia and Eastern Europe to Latin America, grapples with historical denial. Gabriel García Márquez has called it being exiled from memory. The last blow to the last of the Buendía line in *One Hundred Years of Solitude* is the old priest's denial that Colonel Aureliano Buendía fought thirty-two wars and that three thousand workers were gunned down and their bodies thrown into the sea. This is as good an account as any of the denials of actual history that we have been fed. These denials are delivered with straight faces, smug self-assurance, academic credentials, even a barely masked sneer. They spell out for us what exists and what never happened, how things come into being from absolute nothingness and vanish into it at whim, what is decreed directly from heaven and what ascends straight back there... Perhaps it is large parts of the official histories of the twentieth century that ought to be called magic realism. Nonetheless, even if unlike the Buendías the demise of the Iranian people is not recorded in any chronicle, a great deal of the population, inside and out-side the country, has been "exiled from memory" just like that doomed family.

Those exiled Iranians who left the country ran away from the conditions of life in Iran. We ran from isolation, lawlessness, underground living, and daily tor-ment. We ran from threat, constriction, and cultural ex-tinction. To make it short, we ran from something that is the opposite of the freedom to be. Many of us had no intention of becoming immigrants in any country. We spent decades straddling emigration, asylum and exile on one side, and the numbing security of various docu-ments—visas, residencies, citizenships—on the other. We had no plans. We still don't. But we've finally reached the stage where, having had our noses conclusively rubbed in impermanence, we have developed an appreciation for precarious positions. I think we might have something to say about what goes on inside black holes.

One of the pockets within this abyss is what is called "brain drain." This is actually an international space. When I first came to the U.S. as a foreign stu-dent in the 1970s I had a running joke with some fellow undergrad international students about starting a club called International Brain Drain Society. One night, af-ter a few beers, some of us even made little IBDS mem-bership cards. Back then most members of IBDS would have been from the Third World—Africa, Asia, Latin America. (One can easily find long-lost friends in Rober-to Bolaño or Agha Shahid Ali.) And after the fall of the Soviet Union we definitely would have had to open our membership to Russians and Eastern Europeans as well. By then more parts of the world were hemorrhaging brain than not. By now we would be taking in refugees from developed countries.

But I dislike the phrase "brain drain" for two reasons. One, it implies that the countries that we left behind are now suffering from brain deficiency. That's ridiculous; brain is a renewable natural resource. Second, it implies that somehow the brains of emigrants are absorbed into the brain pool of the host countries. That's also ridiculous. Clearly our host countries are much more in need of cheap labor than brain—there's a surplus of the homegrown variety already. But, see, in our naïveté we took our brains seriously.

The American husband of a relative of mine who lived in Iran for a few years in the late sixties told me this joke that circulated among the Americans in Iran at the time:

Question: What happens when all these Iranians who go to the U.S. to study stay there and never come back?
Answer: The average IQ of both countries is lowered.

I can just picture the various American "advisors" and tag-alongs passing on this joke under their breath at glittering dinner parties, holding large plates heaped with sumptuous Iranian food. I wish they had choked on those succulent pieces of kabab they were helping themselves to. But—suffering from an abundance of confidence— had we heard this joke back then we would more likely have dismissed it as American impudence than taken it to heart.

Years later I read a comment by Noam Chomsky that the intelligentsia of the Third World is quite naïve as to exactly how cynical the western elites, including the intelligentsia, are. I agree. That's what I mean when I say that we took our brains too seriously. We took everybody's brains seriously: here, there, everywhere. We thought there was inherent value in the gray matter. Many of us just did not get the message no matter how bluntly it was drummed into our heads: No submission, no prize.

When the American hostages were taken in 1979, I came up with a clever little witticism. "There are two stages to American foreign policy," it went, "crime and prejudice followed by pride and punishment." Crime and prejudice is the stage when the U.S., like other colonial powers before it, is unchallenged in its sense of supremacy and entitlement. Pride and punishment follows when the countries subjected to crime and prejudice presume to assert their sovereignty and independence. (The revolution in 1979 was a declaration of independence of sorts: "When in the course of human events it becomes necessary for one people to dissolve the political bonds which have connected them with another...") In the past four decades a lot of Iranians have had to quietly put up a double resistance: against the derision and punishment of injured American pride on the one hand, and against the hubris and brutality of the Islamic Republic on the other.

The abyss into which my generation slid day by day in Iran was not all that different from the one we experienced outside. If our brains were chewed up and spat out in the west, theirs were spat out in virgin state.

But then again, there is something to be said for crude survival. Once I gave this topic to my freshman composition class in the Bronx: "An unexamined life is not worth living." One of my students put me to shame. "Any kind of life is worth living," she wrote. And as for us, the "burned generation" of more than one generation in Iran, we have perhaps now survived long enough to start crawling out of the black hole. It certainly seems the time has arrived to take a serious look inside the hole—heck, maybe even some of those celebrated gems might turn up, scattered near and far.

Or, as an American professor of mine put it less flatteringly years ago, as soon as the edge of a certain hostility dulls, Iranians will start crawling out of the woodwork in all kinds of places.

Digital Reconstruction

Iraj Kalantari, a renowned architect and brother of one of Iran's renowned painters, Parviz Kalantari, had designed our old house in Tehran. The simple but elaborate design left an impression on discerning people, including a young architect I met years later who was a niece of a later owner. (A mutual friend had mentioned my name and she had asked if I was related to the original owner of that marvelous house.) My parents sold the house shortly before the revolution. The second owner was a rich rug merchant from the bazaar who covered the floors with multiple layers of exquisite rugs, the worth of which far exceeded the price of the house. When my father sold him the house, the rug merchant was so kind as to have our (humble) carpets professionally cleaned into the bargain.

For several years after the revolution my mother was barred from leaving the country. She had schools and ran welfare programs for deaf children and their families, most of whom were too poor to afford tuition or other services. She received public funding for her schools and programs. The reputation of her schools, which were started by her father, and other centers, which were established by her, was impeccable and they served as models for both educational and public-service institutions. Immediately after the revolution, accusations against anyone or any entity successful under the previous regime were rampant, and my mother was accused of being a double agent for CIA and KGB and for channeling public funds to the royal family. One eventful day, to defend herself against these accusations, she called a public meeting at her flagship school. Expecting many of the children's families to show up, chairs were set up in the schoolyard. The walnut tree planted in memory of my grandfather stood in one corner of the yard.

Tension ran high during the meeting. Revolutionary guards from the local *komiteh* trickled in, planting themselves in the audience and resting the butts of their semi-automatics against the back of chairs. Many of them were no more than neighborhood boys with access to guns and they let slip afterwards that they were under instruction not to let my mother speak to the assembly. "You will fall under her spell if you let her speak," they were warned. "She can convince you of anything." To battle against this outcome the crowd became especially vicious, drowning her voice.

At one point the bizarre hostility grew to such an extent that my mother's brother, who had by accident dropped by the school, felt compelled to stand up and speak in her defense. He was quite shocked by what he had stumbled into. He called the walnut tree planted in my grandfather's memory witness to the madness that had created a mob out of the same people who had cried in gratitude when their children were enrolled in the school. He was so angry that the force of his gesture pointing to the walnut tree ripped his watch off his wrist and flung it at the tree. The commotion caused by my uncle's outburst shielded my mother and she was smuggled out through the back door and into hiding. She escaped that day with, if not her life, certainly her liberty.

It was family friends, parents of my old friend Maryam S, who saved her that day and afterwards. Maryam's mother, Pari, who had been at the school meeting, whisked my mother off to the safety of her own mother's house. She took a risk not many would have taken. My mother lived in hiding until with the help of Pari's husband, Ardeshir, a prominent surgeon, the worst charges against her were dropped.

Even after the charges were dropped my mother was not allowed to leave the country. The rest of our family was in the U.S. and to join us after nearly four years, she had to leave Iran illegally. She was smuggled out of the country through the mountains of Kurdistan into Turkey. (Her companions on this trip included a young mother who was kidnapping her own son. This woman's husband had recently died and according to the new laws custody of her son had gone to her deceased husband's family.) It took my mother another two years to finally make her way to the U.S., after a stint as a refugee in France.

After my parents sold our family house they bought a small apartment. It was the proceeds from selling this apartment that financed my mother's escape. She lived alone in this apartment during some of the darkest and bloodiest years after the revolution. The earth had shifted under her feet, she had barely escaped who knows what tragic fate, her family was scattered around the globe, but there were times that my mother mostly missed her old house. She missed walking in and setting down her shopping bags on the kitchen counter. She missed sitting with her glass of tea, looking out the living room window. She missed putting her feet up and opening the daily paper. She missed the muffled sound of rock and roll emanating from her son's closed door. She missed straightening the picture frames on the walls. She missed the fruit trees and rose bushes. She missed her home.

One day, overcome with longing, she took a walk by the old house. On the spur of the moment she rang the bell, introduced herself and asked if she might go inside. The rug-merchant owners, whom she had not seen since the house was sold, were kind and courteous as usual and welcomed her in. The multiple layers of exquisite rugs were still on the floors, some walls had come down and others gone up, but there had been an obvious calamity. Virtually every surface in the house was draped in black cloth. The household was in deep mourning. Two of the family's children, a daughter and a son, had recently been executed within months of each other.

After changing hands a few more times the house was finally demolished and replaced by a highrise in black stone. To me the building looks like a colossal tombstone.

But I digress. Iraj, our architect, is considerably younger than my parents but still part of a certain circle of friends. The summer after my father died he hosted a memorial for him at his house and invited only the closest and oldest friends. The connections between these friends feels ancient—friendships that transcended not just personal histories but a greater history spanning nearly a century, friends like the couple who saved and gave refuge to my mother, friendships sealed by many such episodes… Many of the older people at the memorial also had a history of working together professionally, on projects and in ways of which the next generations would only dream. And they were all very well aware how they had survived by the skin of their teeth. Watching the lively and youthful group, many of them pushing eighty, I thought that a secret gratification we share is the knowledge that not many people in the world know such supra-historical friendships. I think Russians understand this.

Justly proud of his work, for a number of years Iraj had been looking for photographs of our old house in its original form. The photos that any of us might have had have vanished through years of moves from house to house, country to country, and city to city. I always have those photos in the back of my mind whenever I come across any of my family's belongings hastily packed sometime and stored somewhere. But Iraj has finally given up. He said that he is just going to digitally reconstruct the house from the design drawings. "We can even animate it," he said.

What have you done, cont.

There was a collection of stories I remember from my childhood, *Good Stories for Good Children*, published by the old Amir Kabir publishing house. One story left a particularly strong impression on me. It was about a traveler who got ambushed by bandits and murdered after being robbed. The black and white illustration showed a sneering bandit pulling back the man's head by his hair, holding a knife to his throat. The traveler, with terror in his eyes, had his arms raised toward a tree where a group of black birds were perched, looking down upon the scene. The robbers were laughing at their victim who in desperation was taking the birds of the sky witness to the crime.

` The story went on like this: years after killing the man the group of bandits were at the traditional picnic on the 13th day of the new year. Having had a good deal to drink the twittering birds in the trees reminded them of their desperate victim long ago who had taken the birds witness, and they had a laugh at the memory. As it happened, next to them a police detective and his family were picnicking. The detective, hearing the vainglorious confession of the criminals apprehended them, bringing them to justice. It turned out that not only did the birds of the sky bear witness to the crime but they even ended up testifying against the murderers.

The concept of bearing witness is essential to Islam. *I bear witness that there is no God but God and Mohammad is his messenger*: by this recitation you convert to Islam. From the Arabic root *sh.h.d* derive such words as *shaahed* (witness), *shahaadat* (bearing witness, also martyrdom), *shaheed* (martyr, the ultimate bearer of witness), *mashhad* (the place of martyrdom) and *ashhad* (the last prayer to be said before the moment of death).

The first-grade textbook of my parents' generation contained some oddly poetic phrases that my father was fond of reciting: *The starling flew from the tree. The soup grew cold.*

Many starlings who have witnessed the crimes of the past forty years have flown the tree. Some have vanished but some are still perched in nearby trees. I remember back in the 1980s driving on the Parkway stretching the southern border of Evin prison, listening to the silence engulfing the compound. It was deafening. One could hear victims taking the entire universe witness.

The ruins of Rey are close to Tehran. This was another of the old phrases from my parents' elementary school text book. The ruins of Tehran are now close to Rey.

The End

My father died in the spring of 2007 in California. In the last few months of his life the efforts of reading and writing were almost too much for him. The last books he browsed were his own unpublished manuscripts. At age eighty-two he found what he wrote in his sixties "dogmatic" and "naïve." It made me laugh that it takes Middle East politics to make an eighty-year old find his sixty-year old self naïve.

Watching my father surrounded by his manuscripts on his deathbed I was reminded of Rousseau reading his own books at the end of his life. I thought of the good fortune of being able to look back at life through your own writing. When I straightened out my father's bed while he napped on the couch I took peeks into what he was reading in the copystore-bound manuscripts around and under his pillows. Sometimes I would get distracted and stay there reading, trying to imagine things through the eyes of a man whose life was coming to an end. "It's a good thing some of these were never published," my father said when he caught me reading, thwarting my efforts to glimpse into the mind of a dying man. "They're not very good." It delighted me that he remained sharp and unsentimental to the end.

My mother and I brought some of my dad's ashes to scatter in Iran. We wanted to pay his last tribute to the mountains where he had spent some of the happiest times of his life. We did not make a ceremony of it because he would have cringed at the idea.

Marjan drove us to the mountains. She is my oldest friend. We were friends as infants, like our brothers were before we came along. There is a preverbal bond between us—what I imagine prehistoric feels like. Having lost her own father not too long ago, Marjan had just the right combination of personal experience and irreverence for the occasion. We chatted as she drove on new highways that were completely unknown to me. Our mothers talked quietly in the back seat.

I told Marjan that in honor of my father's love of Khayyam I had half a mind to mix some of his ashes with pottery clay and make a cup. "Glaze it and drink vodka out of it—*tagari*," I said, only partly joking.

We both thought about it for a minute. "I don't think one should drink vodka out of one's parents," Marjan finally declared.

When we left the new highway behind and as the car climbed up the mountain road in low gear we caught sight of a beautiful white horse galloping ahead. In a minute there was an old pickup truck behind us with two guys hanging from its sides, gesticulating to us to pull over. We let them pass and in another minute they caught up with the tired horse. One of the men jumped down and with a little struggle managed to grab the horse by its mane and turn it back. We caught up with them and stopped. Marjan rolled down her window and I snapped some pictures. "Ran away from the stable…" explained the guy leading the horse past our car. As Marjan engaged him in her trademark loopy prattle, the horse jerked its neck in a last attempt to break free. Its sweaty gray mane glistened in the sun and its eyes flashed.

We picked a spot by a brook, overlooking a valley dotted with a village on one side and mountain peaks looking deceptively close on the other. It was a windy day. The wind snatched my father's ashes out of our hands before any reached the brook. It threw them back into our faces and dusted our clothes.

I mixed a pinch of ash with some dirt in my hand. I felt the gritty mixture of pebbles and bits of my father's bones on my palm. I suppose this is what I believe in. It's the only return there is.

My father loved Khayyam. The closer he got to death, and the more his lived and imagined lives mixed in his memory, the more he communed with two men: the eminent scholar and poet Parviz Natel Khanlari, with whom he had studied and worked, and Khayyam. My mother chose this Khayyam couplet to send to friends with a picture of my father engrossed in reading a book:

> *I saw him astride the planet earth—*
> *No blasphemy, no Islam, no religion, nor the world,*
> *No right, no truth, no law, and no certitude—*
> *Who in the two worlds has such gall?*

COUNTRY POP

O n the way home she drove by a sandy-haired, lanky
boy carrying a guitar case. A wide-rimmed hat dan-
gled from the straps around his neck, partly covering his
backpack. When she caught another glimpse of him in
the rear view mirror she saw that there was also a banjo
strapped across his chest.

She was putting the groceries away when there
was a knock at the door. She opened the door holding a
head of lettuce.

"Hi Robin, I'm Tom."

It was the boy she had passed, his guitar and banjo resting against the wall, the pack still on his back.

Gary had told her about Tom: he had a summer
gig at a country bar in town and would be going to LA
in the fall to look for recording work. If Robin would let
him stay with her a couple of days until he found a place
to stay... Sure, Robin had said. Gary was her friend Denise's boyfriend and Tom had been Gary's friend in high
school.

Tom walked in. Robin's house was a low-ceil-
inged cottage in the back of a bigger house. It was a small
space for Tom at his height and with his gear. But he glided in, lifted the hat over his head, unburned himself of

the backpack, and arranged everything as unobtrusively as he could in a corner. Robin stood at the door a bit too still and a bit too long, watching him. Tom moved with a quiet grace at once bashful and confident. His pack, his sleeping bag, the guitar case, his body released a scent of freshly chopped wood. "I'm sorry to take up so much space," he said. "And it's sure getting warm," he wiped his forehead with his sleeve.

"Not at all," Robin motioned to the couch and pulled up a chair herself. He sat down awkwardly, still looking overheated. "Why don't you cool off first," she said as she got up again to fetch him a towel. "Wash up and I'll get you a drink." Then she thought, I'll just make a meal, he's probably hungry. She was busy cooking when Tom walked into the tiny kitchen in a fresh but crumpled t-shirt and hair slicked back with a wet comb. The smell of freshly chopped wood wafted from him more distinctly.

They sat at the kitchen table, opened cold beers, ate, lingered and talked: how long his bus trip took, how hot it got on the way, how he found this gig in town, whom he'd be playing with, friend in LA who could hook him up with session work...

"Gary said you're moving by the end of the summer too," he said. "Where to?"

"Graduate school," she said.

"What's your major?"

"English literature."

"You're going to be a teacher?"

"Probably."

He stepped into the living room to be out of her way as she cleared the table, and sat on the floor by the turntable, flipping through Robin's albums: mostly rock and roll, a few jazz and blues, and some classical.

"What kind of music do you play?" Robin asked as she came in and sat on the couch.

"I don't know," he said. "I play whatever the band I play with plays. Or whatever the club wants."

"But what do you play for yourself?"

"I don't know, " he said again. "I just play."

"What kind of music do you like?"

"All kinds. I like the music you've got here."

Robin was curious to hear him but she didn't want to impose. Her phone in the bedroom rang. It had to do with her housing arrangement at graduate school so she had to stay on the phone for a while. While she was talking on the phone she heard Tom take out his guitar, gently strumming and tuning it. Then he played a few notes and softly slipped into a lick.

Having been put on hold, Robin sat on her bed, holding the phone to her ear, listening to the sound coming from the living room. Tom was just playing around, picking up a melody, slipping into another, expanding, stopping abruptly, picking up another phrase, speeding it up, slowing down, exaggerating, making jokes... There was something out of the ordinary about his sound. It was warm and cool at the same time. It was gentle and soft with a peculiar strength. It was an encompassing sound. It seemed to touch all corners of the house and fill the space with deep resonance. He engaged the space, as it were, making it ring with his intention.

When she went back to the living room he lowered the volume of his playing and faded it out, not wavering for a moment.

He looked up from his guitar. Robin's heart jumped.

"I guess I play mostly country, that's what pays

around here," he said. "I grew up listening to it. Country, folk, old ballads, that's what people play. But I listen to the radio a lot."

"Play more," Robin said. "Please do."

"I don't want to bore you."

"Oh please…"

"OK then, but tell me to stop when you've had enough."

He started to play again, louder this time. And he played and played. He modulated from key to key and melody to melody, some from familiar tunes some not, and as he relaxed into his music, longer and faster riffs poured from his sliding and picking fingers. He played with the boldness and imagination of rock and roll, the simplicity of old-country folk tunes, and even the simultaneous restraint and abandon of flamenco. He could play anything. And as he played, the unassuming country boy transformed into a deeply absorbed virtuoso.

Tom was in absolute control of what and how much sound he projected. Music enveloped the space around them but never overwhelmed it. Robin had never been in the presence of this caliber of musicianship. She was awestruck. He played with a brilliant but subdued sound, engaging but not overpowering.

He finally put the guitar down. They were both quiet. To make conversation he started flipping through Robin's albums again. He smiled at some of them, then playfully picked up his guitar once again—"I do this sometimes at the end of a sets and people like it," he said. "It's for entertainment"—a few chords and he slipped into the good-natured and plaintive voice of Paul McCartney, cooing one of his hits. Then he changed tunes and put Bob Dylan's gravelly hiss in his voice, mimicking Dylan's simultaneously distant and in-your-face sound, chewing up and spitting out his words.

"You sure are so good at this!" Robin couldn't help exclaiming.

"This is how I taught myself, by copying people who were good at it."

"Now sing something in your own voice."

He put the guitar away, in its case this time, and flipped the latch shut. "Another time," he said.

Soon after that they went to bed, she in her bedroom and he on the living room floor in his sleeping bag. Robin flipped on the light by her bed and took up her novel. She had assigned herself to finish reading all of Trollope that summer. She propped up a fat pocket edition and picked up where she had left off. But she was distracted. She read passages over and over again but was not absorbing them. She turned off the light, lied back and stared at the ceiling. The street light flickered through the branches of a tree. The light is too distracting, she thought, and got up and shut the curtains. Lying back down her heart started pounding. She tossed and turned. She listened to the rustling of Tom's sleeping bag in the other room. It felt very hot. She got up again and opened the window to let the night air in. It was fresh and cool and suddenly she felt so alive. She was not sleepy at all. She wanted to go out and do things. She felt hungry, wished she could go out to eat with friends and listen to music.

Then she sat back on the bed and suddenly felt cold. The night air was getting too cool. She shut the window half way and got under the covers. A rush of anxiety came over her. She had graduated from college, was on her way to do some more serious studying, then what…? What in the world for? Give up her little house in the town she had gotten to know and where she had friends? Why break everything up and go to a new place? Who was she and what was she doing? She heard Tom get up and quietly slide open the living room window. So he's too hot too, she thought. I better not go to the other room because he has probably kicked off his sleeping bag and is sleeping almost naked. She turned her light back on and tried to read once more. She got distracted again. I want a piping hot chop and roast potatoes—she was reading about Plantagenet Palliser eating after a long day at work. Would be fun to dress up in all those fineries— she was imagining Glencora—great hair she has… Nah, this is not working, she said to herself, then put away the novel and turned off the light. The night seemed interminable. It was nearly dawn when she finally slipped into a fitful and dream-filled sleep.

She woke up late. When she went to the living room Tom was not there. She panicked for a split second. Then she saw his sleeping back rolled up and stashed behind her couch. She then actually felt glad that he had stepped out. She could use the time to get herself together and straighten up her room. She was drinking her coffee at the kitchen table when Tom knocked gently and walked in.

"Good morning," he said. "I went out to see what it's like around here."

"Not much going on," she said. "Coffee?"

Again they lingered for a long time at the kitchen table. Then Robin said that she could take him by the club where he would be playing to talk to the manager and arrange things. He was not to start until Friday night, after which he could board with the other players nearby. After touching base at the club she took him to her favorite hangout. It was a semi-abandoned warehouse that had been turned into a little café and bookstore at one end and a makeshift bar and club at the other. The Warehouse, as it was generally called, was mostly a hang-out for college kids, where they collected in the evenings and jammed with fly-by-night musicians. The acoustics were not good and the seats threadbare and beat-up, but the kids didn't care. They just wanted to play and hear music. It was a time when music was everywhere, a good time to be a musician.

Both Robin and Tom on tight budgets, they went home to make dinner. Robin was happy to cook while Tom played. She could see from the corner of her eyes that he was unaware of anything else when he played. She felt a pang of insecurity. Then she poked fun of her-self by thinking of the line in Gigi: "She is not. Thinking. Of me." She managed to find her bearing but could not entirely control the haywire beating in her heart.

They ate, listened to some records, chatted, but the whole time Robin wanted to cry. There was a lump, a constriction in her throat. Tom was not at ease like the night before either. He seemed troubled and did not reach for his guitar. Late at night, without saying more than just goodnight, Robin went to her bedroom.

Tom followed her. Again, without saying any-thing, they sat on the bed side by side. Tom laid his hand on her bare arm. The touch of his fingers, a little cal-loused from the steel strings of his guitar, felt like kiss-es on her skin. She looked into his eyes up close. It was so easy to do that. He looked back with his gentle and earnest gaze. Then he closed his eyes and bent over her. His lips touched hers and they were warm and cool like his playing. She let herself sink back into the pillows as he nuzzled her with the same bashful confidence of his steps. His embrace was as encompassing as his sound and his skin glided over hers like silk. He filled her with abandon and awe.

That night they fell deeply asleep in each other's arms and woke up not having budged all night. In the morning when Robin first opened her eyes she felt a delicious warmth. She did not move but turned her face to Tom. His eyes were closed but he gave her shoulders a squeeze. This is so easy, thought Robin, this is how it's supposed to be. In a little while she stroked his hair, planted a kiss on his brow, and got up. He curled up and went back to sleep. In the kitchen sunlight was streaming in. I am so happy, she thought, how lovely I feel... She wanted to jump and run and play. "I love summer," she said out loud.

Tom did not leave to stay with the other band members. They spent their days at home, she mostly reading, he, playing–not practicing. "I don't practice," he corrected her. "I just play."

"So let me see what you're interested in," he said one lazy afternoon after lunch. He ran his hand over the row of her Penguin paperbacks. "Lots of foreign authors... how do you say this, Cheykov?"

"Chekhov," she corrected him. "Russian."

"A lot of Russian books–you like Russian?"

"I love Russian literature but I read it in English. I wish I knew Russian."

"Why don't you learn it?"

"To really learn a language you have to live in the country and it's very hard to go to Russia right now. Especially to live there long enough to learn the language well."

"Why? Because it's communist?"

"Yup," she said. "But the literature is still incredible in English. You want me to read you a little?'

"Yes," he said and looked more closely at the books. He picked Turgenev: "*Sketches from a Hunter's Album*—read from this. I grew up hunting."

Robin opened the volume and flipped through it. "How about this hunting scene?"—she read:

> In spring, a quarter of an hour before sunset, you go into the woods with your gun but not your dog. You look for a place for yourself near a thicket. You look around some more, inspect your gun, exchange winks with your companion...

Tom smiled, listening.

> A quarter of an hour passes. The sun sinks below the horizon but it is still light. The air is fresh, the sky is clear, there is the chatter of birds, the tender grass glows emerald green. You wait.

"This is good," Tom said, still smiling. Robin read on:

> Gradually the woods start to darken from their deep interior. The last crimson rays of the sun slide up the trunk of the trees, licking the lower branches, then all the way to the top. Slowly the very tips of the trees darken. The pale pink of the sky becomes a dark blue. The subtle but powerful scent of the woods creeps up on you and the warm and damp breath of the trees engulf you. The birds seem to fall asleep, but not all at once. First the finches fall silent, then the robins, and after a while the little yellow buntings. The woods grow darker and darker...

Robin fell silent and looked at Tom with a suppressed

chuckle. A bit of a frown played on his brow.

"This is very nice," he said. "The writing has so much power behind it."

"You like it? I'm glad. But let me show you even greater power." She got up and fetched *Anna Karenina:*

> Spring was slow in coming. The weather had been clear and frosty the last few weeks before Lent. The ice thawed in the sun at daytime but at night there was seven degrees of frost again. The icy crust on the snow was so hard that carts went everywhere without needing to keep to the road. At Easter there was still snow on the ground. Then suddenly, on Easter Monday, a warm wind rose, clouds gathered, and then for three days and nights a mild, warm rain fell.
>
> On Thursday the wind ceased and a thick gray mist covered the land, like a cloak hiding the changing mysteries beneath. Piercing the impenetrable mist, melted snow gushed forth and the ice on the river cracked and was swept downstream in turbid, frothing torrents. Then the following Monday evening the mist lifted, the clouds broke up into puffs of white, the sky cleared, and spring finally arrived.

Tom was silent. Robin wondered if she had lost him. He then repeated, more thoughtfully this time: "There is so much power behind this writing."

"You think about power a lot?" Robin teased him.

"Well, you have to put strength into what you're doing, otherwise it's no good."

"I know what you mean. My regret is that I can't read this stuff in Russian, it must be so much more powerful in the original."

"What difference does it make?"

"Well, it's not exactly like music but language has a power of its own. Sometimes the simpler the language the stronger it is. I'll show you."

She fetched the collected works of Shakespeare that she had picked up in a second hand bookstore and sat next to him. She liked the smell of the leather binding and passed the book to him to get a sniff. He took a whiff and chuckled: "It just smells old."

"Have you read much poetry?" she asked.

He looked a little embarrassed. "I don't understand poetry, I dropped out of high school."

"It doesn't matter. You speak English, don't you?" She tapped on an open page:

> *Shall I compare thee to a summer's day?*
> *Thou art more lovely and more temperate*

"What's not to understand here?" she turned to him. He nodded. She continued:

> *Rough winds do shake the darling buds of May,*
> *And summer's lease hath all too short a date*

"What does the last line mean?" he asked.

"What do you think it means?"

"That summer is too short."

"Correct," she said. "With poetry a lot of times you get it without understanding how it is that you get it. Just listen:

> *Sometime too hot the eye of heaven shines,*
> *And often is his gold complexion dimm'd;*
> *And every fair from fair sometime declines,*
> *By chance, or nature's changing course, untrimm'd*

She paused. He kept his gaze on the page and was silent. She went on:

But thy eternal summer shall not fade,
Nor lose possession of that fair thou ow'st;
Nor shall death brag thou wander'st in his shade,
When in eternal lines to time thou grow'st

"Now how is this for simplicity," she read on:

So long as men can breathe, or eyes can see,
So long lives this, and this gives life to thee

Then she fell silent and waited.

"You know what's really interesting to me?" Tom broke the silence. "You don't really have to add anything to words. You just let them speak for themselves. You can do that in singing too."

"I still haven't heard your real voice," Robin said.

"Another time," he said again and walked away.

Their days fell into a languid and happy pattern. They woke up late in the mornings. She read, he played, they made occasional trips to the store, ate, and then she gave him a ride to his evening gig at the club. He was usually done by midnight when Robin picked him up and they dropped by the Warehouse where the kids had already assembled to jam. That's where Robin finally heard Tom sing.

Word had spread about this new serious musician in town. Players from all over town started showing up, lugging their instruments, or sitting at the rinky-dink piano at the Warehouse to play with Tom. He laughed and picked, dueled on his guitar and banjo, and wowed everyone with his singing—and not just his imitations. Sometimes after he had played everyone else to the ground he picked up his guitar and accompanied himself on a song. They were not original songs but he had a way of making them his own. His voice claimed the music and his delivery the words.

His voice was extraordinary: the range and strength, the clarity, the tenderness, the quiet confidence, and above all the golden timbre. It went straight to the heart and was pumped into the blood stream. It encountered no resistance. It acknowledged no resistance. He sang in a voice so clear and so strong that a hush fell over the entire large space of the warehouse. When he unleashed the full range of his gleaming tenor, holding those high notes without a quiver, the listeners couldn't help but to hold their breath and look at each other in wonder.

One night when Tom was in rare form and the audience was hushed with rapt attention, Robin watched him look right through her as he sang. She marveled at the control he had over his voice, projecting it toward every inch of the big warehouse, challenging, as it were, the bad acoustics, the awful echo. She basked in the warmth and fullness of the musical space he created—and then became aware of the dark emptiness outside, the silence that threatened to devour the music inside. Then her attention returned to Tom. This is a larger than life talent, she thought to herself, it can't be stopped. She felt sad—tinged, sigh, with envy, and even intimations of jealousy.

They drove home in silence that night and went to bed later than usual, but Robin could not fall asleep. She tossed and turned and fought the urge to take repeated deep breaths. Her head was full of sounds: the car engine idling as she waited for Tom outside his bar, the thump of the guitar and banjo cases thrown on the back seat, the car doors slamming, the din and chatter at the Warehouse as people moved from the café over to the bar, new people coming in, the pulling up of chairs, laughter, instruments being tuned. A few chords, a few hummed notes, a little rest for Tom, and the amateurs warming up... Then the sounds grew louder in her ears, images more distinct: instruments and voices joining in, tempo picking up, Tom unfolding his arms, smiling, picking up the banjo, lending the strength of his voice, harmonizing, putting down the banjo, picking up the guitar, breaking in with wild riffs that made everyone hoot and holler... All these echoed in Robin's head as she lay in bed with wide-open eyes.

She finally left the bed and sat at the kitchen table with a glass of water in front of her. Her mind was a jumble of sounds and images but somehow it didn't feel like random chaos. It was as if something lurking in the heart of that noise was trying to break through. She sat for a long time trying to decipher what that something was. It was no message, it had no meaning, it could not be put in words. It was more like a quiet spot of light that was trying to shine through. It was an indecipherable awareness. She just sat there, giving in to that spot of light. She was very still. Eventually the noise started withdrawing into the background of her mind. She sipped her water and continued to look out the window at the darkness. Her rooms never got quite dark at night. Light from a street lamp some distance from the house filtered through the leaves of an aspen tree, throwing fluttering patterns on her walls. She never got tired of watching the dance of the leaves. It is rare that there is no breeze, no movement, she thought.

Eventually the kitchen chair felt uncomfortable. She left to lie down on the couch. On the floor next to Tom's guitar she saw a book face down, open to page three of a story he had picked out to read. Some days before, Tom had said that he should try to read some of her books now that she had heard so much of his music. "Pick any," Robin had said, and Chekhov's "Lady with a Lapdog" had caught his eye. He had chuckled at the title and asked what it was about. "It's a love story," Robin said. "Love of a dog?" he joked. Then he added out of the blue: "You should get a little dog." "Someday I will," she said.

Well, he apparently had not gotten far into the story. She knew how whenever he tried to make himself do anything it would slowly be put away, the guitar picked up, and slow muted notes would follow. The fact is the guy practiced all the time. He said that he didn't practice, he just played. That's right. Talented people just play. One night he had gotten into a guitar duel with another player and he had burst into the Wilhelm Tell overture on his guitar, accelerating the tempo until the other guy's fingers nearly bled. Robin was flabbergasted: "How in the world did you learn to play that?"

"From a record," he said, "I don't read music." Obviously the guy had spent copious amounts of his life practice/playing. "I listened to so much Django Rhinehard that I wore out my friends' records."

Robin stretched out on the couch, clasping her hands behind her head. She closed her eyes. A flutter rose from her heart and settled in her throat in a constriction. She felt it like a flickering light.

After a while she picked up the volume resting on the floor. There's no putting down a Chekhov story when you start one. She read it through and remembered how a long time ago—she was quite young—she had given herself the advice never to forget how great Chekhov is. Too bad we don't acknowledge the talent of reading, she said to herself, because some people are just talented readers. And she was once again reminded of how great Chekhov is. The little flickering light travelling her body expanded as she read. It filled her with the glow of moonlight: soft, unimposing, vast. The light silenced the last of the noisy clutter in her head. She closed her eyes and was soon asleep.

The next morning Tom seemed a little troubled. "Why didn't you come to bed last night?" he asked.

"I couldn't fall asleep and didn't want to wake you up."

"It felt bad waking up alone in the bed."

They were both quiet for a while. But Tom did not seem any less troubled.

"Come to LA with me," he said.

Robin suddenly felt very sad. "LA is not my world," she said. "I don't belong there."

"I don't belong there either. I'm just going there to make it as a musician."

"We're headed in different directions," Robin said quietly.

Tom looked hurt. "All these books you read make you sad," he said. "I couldn't even read that story about the lady and her dog, it was too sad."

"You didn't get very far into the story, how did you know it was sad?"

"It was sad from the first word."

"It's not like there's no sadness in your music," she said.

Tom didn't say anything. Then he got up while still holding and patting her hand. "Will you think about it? LA?"

Summer went by quickly as it always does.

One hot dusty day toward the end of summer they drove to the mountains for reprieve. With the elevation came a cool breeze. Fall was in the air, there was no mistaking it. As they snaked up the mountain road the breeze gathered momentum and it soon packed a punch. They rolled up their windows. High above them clumps of white cloud rushed by and clung together somewhere in the far distance. Still, the sun shone in full strength and blasted through the breaks in the clouds. Once they reached the pine treeline they stopped to spread out a picnic. They sat side by side on a tattered blanket with Tom's guitar between them. Neither felt like talking. There was a lot to listen to.

A posse of small dark birds flitted in and out of the branches, letting out abrupt broken chirps. Some other bird species obscured in the rustling bushes emitted persistent squeaks, while a couple of pretty little things in plain view insisted on contributing their cheerful twittering. Attempts by faraway songbirds trilling happily were punctuated by bursts of vexed and alarmed squeals nearby. The wayward wind in the trees suddenly whipped up and ruthlessly wiped out all other sound. Then a squeal or two rose in objection from a winged source, appropriately concealed. A blue-black crow, perched on the top branch of a lone poplar, seemed to listen with mock attentiveness. There's quite a little drama going on here, Robin thought to herself, it's a story. All the while a doleful and scarcely audible murmur of another bird carried on and on in the distance. Robin thought, I don't know birds at all, I could not name a single one.

Tom braced against a boulder, whistling to the birds, the twittering ones. Some of them trilled back, oth-

ers fell abruptly silent, and yet others persisted in shriek-
ing in shrill unison. He took out his guitar and started
picking out identifiable notes in the birds' calls. A lone
bird hiding in a tree a few paces over offered a few longer
and almost coherent phrases. Tom picked up the cue and
embellished it. The originator of the melody fell curiously silent. Then a sudden gush of wind suppressing a
howl took Tom's attention away. He strummed a couple
of chords approximating a response to the howl. Then a
dull growl of thunder barged in, announcing its distant
presence. Tom took that on with a series of dissonant
chords in a bold attempt to rival the ferocity, and then
slowly started to weave back in the disparate cries and
sweet trilling of the other sound-makers in the trees. The
cacophony of bird, wind, and guitar seemed to stir the
air even more and almost willfully trespass the silence of
the woods. All this while the distant doleful song droned
on.

     This is music like never was nor will be again, ran
through Robin's mind, and she suddenly became aware
that the clouds had clumped thicker together, closing out
the sun. The wind was blowing hard, echoing dryly in the
thicket of thirsty, late summer branches. Tom too looked
up and gave a startled whistle. "We better get going," he
said. "It's going to come down any second." As they hur-
riedly packed up and loaded the car, fat, emphatic drops
of rain fell on their heads.

     It rained hard on their drive back home but in
town it was still summer and sunny. Soon after that day
Robin headed east and Tom west.

The first couple of years in LA were not easy for Tom. With no permanent address and the odd hours he kept, phone calls between Tom and Robin trickled off. By the time he made a name for himself by playing any random gig in town and showing his abilities, they had fallen completely out of touch.

Eventually Tom landed a lucrative niche with a loosely defined group of studio musicians and pretty soon he was in high demand for recording sessions. He played guitar and sang harmony on many albums, playing second fiddle, so to speak, to many stars in the music world. His impeccable ear, technical facility, and musical versatility paid off. But he knew he could do more. And, lo and behold, it didn't take long before his cover of a not particularly successful song made him a big name practically overnight. He knew how to make a song his own. That first single quickly became the number one hit on both country and pop charts.

It is not easy to follow a great hit with another, but Tom did it. And another and another. He knew how to pick them. His string of successful singles made him a sure business bet and he soon signed with a famous record company. But the sweet record deal changed his music. The label produced arrangements slathered with the sugary swoon of the string section that muddled the sound of many other artists under its contract. It wasn't just bad taste; it made everyone's music sound the same.

Robin certainly heard Tom's initial singles. There was no escaping them, they blared from every radio station. But once the schlocky arrangements overpowered Tom's music she lost interest. She bought none of his LPs and soon the only time she encountered any sign of him was on the front page of tabloids in the supermarket.

Tom Camden had become a bona fide celebrity, complete with drinking and drug problems and turgid love affairs.

Robin was immersed in her own world. For her those were the years of papers and exams and departmental politics—but mostly papers: papers written, given, discussed, defended, graded, improved, expanded, discarded. And as the paper mill churned, friendships formed over heady dinners, academic landmarks reached or abandoned, careers blossomed or stalled, moves across states considered, partnerships and marriages made and unmade, and conferences, publications, meetings, colleagues, chairs, lots of students, a few children, old parents, divorce, split houses, children gone, plans for retirement—the usual stuff.

She was now living in a small house, her children off to college, her tenure long secured, her marriage dissolved. Now I want to write, she had decided. Tired of talk, of intellectual bustle and overblown enthusiasm over the minutiae of academe. Time to liberate oneself. Life was not bad at all.

One rainy April afternoon Robin's little dog ran to the door barking and jumping up and down. When the bell rang she opened the door.

"Hello Robin."

She was speechless for a moment. "Tom Camden!" she finally exclaimed. "What in the world...?"

As they stood looking at each other the little dog ran in circles around Tom, yapping happily, galloping to fetch toys to leave at his feet. When they recovered themselves they followed the dog inside as it dashed to move his toys to where they were headed. "What a friendly dog," Tom said, "hospitable like you."

Robin was still a bit tongue tied. She helped Tom hang up his wet coat and showed him to the sitting room. They sat down, both on the edge of their seats, a bit stiffly.

"Well, well, well," Robin said. "What are you doing here?"

"Taking a break from engagements. I hope it's ok to come to you."

"Of course," she said, "of course."

They sat quietly, looking at each other, smiling, still uncomfortable. Tom did not smell of freshly chopped wood anymore. He had a nice smell of something like cologne mixed with a little tobacco.

"So how did you find me?" she asked.

"Gary and Denise."

"You're still in touch with them?"

"I've always been—well, sort of." He looked away, more uncomfortable than before. "They stayed in touch with me. There were years when I lost contact with a lot of people."

"I guess that sort of thing happens when you become famous."

"Famous," he repeated mechanically. "When you become famous, as you call it, you become very busy. Remaining famous is a lot of work."

"I'm sure," Robin smirked. She was partly amused and partly sarcastic and didn't try to hide it. "I'm sure you've got stories to tell."

"How are you?" Tom took no offence at the sarcasm. "How have you been?"

"I'm alright. Decent job. Divorced. Kids gone… Want a drink?"

"I shouldn't drink," Tom said. "Cigarettes are my

only vice now and I'm trying to keep that to a minimum so I roll my own."

"You smoke now?" Robin asked, still not knowing what to say.

"Not a lot," he said. "I have to be careful of my voice. But I needed something to help with quitting worse stuff. I needed a crutch.'

"Worse stuff?"

"Alcohol, amphetamines, cocaine, that sort of thing."

"Oh yes I heard. I read, rather."

He looked down and smiled. "I'm sure," he said.

"So smoking helps?"

"It does. It's like meditation for me. Don't laugh."

Robin wasn't laughing. He continued: "Smoking is a ritual. Finding a quiet place, rolling tobacco, licking the paper, taking deep breaths. Then when I put out the stub it's nice sitting quietly by myself for a moment, my head a little buzzed, my mind empty. It's restful."

"I have to tell you something," he changed the subject. "I stalked you a couple of days before ringing your doorbell. "

"Stalked me?" Robin chuckled. "What in the world for?"

"I needed some kind of reassurance before ringing your doorbell. I didn't know how you might receive me."

"Receive you, Mr. famous celebrity?"

"Even when you're famous you can't take everything for granted, you know."

"So what reassurance made you ring my doorbell?"

"Your little dog."

Robin looked at him, puzzled. "My dog?"

"Catching sight of you with your little dog gave me the courage. It felt like a sign."

"What are you talking about?" Robin was still puzzled.

"Remember that story I never finished that summer I stayed with you? The Lady with the Lapdog? I finally read it. It had a peculiar effect on me. I can't quite say what. Anyway, the guy in the story stalked the lady too!"

"Peculiar effect!" Robin chuckled. "That's Chekhov for you."

"It may be a little crazy but for some reason I always remembered that story. But all I remembered was that it was about a woman with a little dog, by a Russian writer. I asked around until I found it."

"Whom did you ask?" Robin was curious.

"There are literary types in Hollywood, you know."

"Indubitably!" she laughed. "So did you read the entire story this time?"

"I did–not that I understood very much. But I did like it somehow. And when I saw you with a little dog I took it as the sign I was looking for."

"This is wonderful!" Robin let out a laugh. "I love it!"

"I thought you might. That's what gave me courage."

Robin got up and without even thinking about it gave him a kiss square on his lips. "I love Chekhov," she laughed again, "I always knew I could count on him. How long are you here for?"

"I have a few days."

"You want to stay with me?"

"Can I?"

They looked at each other, smiling. The gentle eagerness was still in his eyes. Then he hesitated. "I hope you don't think I'm using you as a crutch."

Robin sat down again and leaned back against the cushions. "Nothing wrong with serving as an occasional crutch," she said.

Later one of Tom's guys delivered his suitcase and a guitar from the hotel where the crew was staying. Robin made room in her closet to hang up his clothes. When he opened his suitcase she identified another ingredient of his scent. "Lavender," she smiled as she took a whiff of his neatly folded shirts.

"My housekeeper irons them with lavender water. My ex taught her. The housekeeper came with me after the divorce. It's a lot easier to keep house for me than my ex with three kids and a big house. I'm on tour a lot."

Robin watched him unpack, then helped arrange his toiletries in the bathroom. Sandalwood shaving soap, that was another ingredient of his scent.

After putting his stuff away they sat side by side on the bed. She breathed him in. It was wonderful to see him again. And after all those years and across worlds apart she felt oddly at ease. She turned to face him directly and looked into his eyes. It was still easy to do that. In the years past she had only made that kind of eye contact with her children.

"Was your divorce bitter?" she asked.

"My ex was bitter. She took the kids, the house, and most of my money. I don't blame her, I wasn't much of a husband or father."

"With your boozing and drugging and womanizing you mean…?"

"So what about you? I heard about your divorce from Denise. How did that happen?"

"Well! How can I put it in a nutshell?" Robin took a breath. "I felt drained, expended, consumed. You raise a family, you teach, you try to make a happy, meaningful life for everybody. You feel you must live your life in a way that is an affirmation of good things, the right things—that takes a lot of work too, you know. I'm exhausted."

"What about the marriage?"

"Marriage! It always starts with the promise of a happy partnership, doesn't it? But for me it slowly became more draining than nourishing. I can't say how it started, it happened so gradually. But suddenly I realized I had to make a choice between going down the road to shriveling up and dying or bursting out of my skin one last time." She looked up at Tom with a smile: "Which one would you choose?"

Tom paused. "I don't know. I guess I don't see things that way."

"Me, I needed a little solitude to find my strength again."

"I got a sense of your strength the summer we spent together. You don't encounter that very often."

They fell silent again. "Let me make dinner for you," Robin said as she got up.

Later they sat at the kitchen table, dirty dishes and half-empty glasses before them, not saying much. It was easy to be silent together. Decades pass and they merely feel like visits to other countries, Robin was thinking. New places, new people, new sights, new routines.

A travel through space but not time. The way she saw it time only changed the place and looks of things.

Tom broke the silence: "I don't mean to act important but did you listen to my music?"

"I heard the first few singles but I didn't really follow you after that."

"You didn't like my music," he said. "Is that why you never got in touch with me?"

"It did not even occur to me to get in touch with you. I'm not a groupie."

Tom smiled: "No one would mistake you for that!" Then he added: "I should have gotten in touch with you. But I got caught in quite a whirlwind—not that it's over now. Anyhow, falling out of touch with people who have touched you is a bad thing."

"Falling out of touch… That's a curious expression, isn't it? It implies that the minute you touch again all distance is traversed."

"Is it?"

"In a way, I guess," she said, and she thought for a moment. "But catching up is a different thing."

"What is catching up? Telling everything that has happened?"

"That can't be done, can it? I don't really know what catching up is. I'll think about it."

Tom took her hand and kissed it. They eventually got up, cleared the table, and went to bed without saying much.

To be lying again in the arms of the golden-voiced and silken-skinned boy of your youth, how lovely is that? Robin thought. She breathed in his new well-heeled scent. His body was heavier, his skin tanned, the hair on his arms and chest a bit coarse. But the touch of his guitarist fingertips still stung a little and his arms engulfed her with the old self-assurance. And the sweet sound of his voice still wreaked havoc in her heart.

He fell asleep holding on to her but she was not sleepy. She lied awake enjoying the bliss. It was a peculiar feeling of peace, one tinged with an elusive and gentle bite. She felt the old flutter rise from her heart and softly land in her throat. She gave herself over to the familiar constriction and she thought, he can sing through that constriction, it's what makes that tearful country sound. Then she smiled to herself, too bad there's not much *I* can do with that constriction. Then for what seemed like a long time she lied in bed listening to his regular breathing and following the impulses that traveled between the outermost layers of her skin and deep inside her bones, her brain, her heart. Gradually all sensations fell away, the embrace of emptiness engulfed her as it travelled from the periphery to her core, and she fell asleep.

The next few days Robin made trips to the university for classes and office hours while Tom stayed put, avoiding outings and enjoying anonymity. Silence was fine but there was curiosity between them.

"So, tell me the truth, what did you really think of my music?" Tom asked as some point. "Were there any songs you liked?"

Robin paused. She did not quite know how to explain.

"I love your singing," she said. "I hear a lot of things in your voice. You have a great gift and fantastic technique. It's impossible not to hear these things."

"But...?" He asked.

"Except your very first hit I hated the arrangement of your songs. It ruined them for me."

"That first one was just a demo tape. My producer released it as it was because he knew how serious I was about picking my own material. It was actually a fluke that I had total artistic control over it."

"Why did you relinquish creative control after that?"

"I signed with a label and then it was the producer who was in charge of the mixing. I recorded the vocal and instrumental tracks and he later applied his lush string arrangements…"

"Lush? You call that lush?" Robin blurted out. "That string section regurgitation, that orchestra vomit…?"

Now Tom let out a laugh. "You sure have a way with words!"

"That's my job, but don't change the subject!" Robin interjected. "I hated that schlock orchestra playing behind you. It is like putting salt in tea, globs of it. It just makes it undrinkable, no matter how fragrant the tea."

"Well my dear the fact is that the music business is more business than music. Once you're signed with a label they're in charge."

"I've heard about that label of yours. It had a uniform sound that could ruin anybody, even Nat King Cole. They gave everyone that same awful sound, like adding the same artificial flavor to every food. Everything had the same bad taste."

"It wasn't just that one label. Early Elvis, with just guitar, base and drums, had a dynamite, raw sound. He was never as sensational when a full-blown band played behind him."

"I imagine your contract ran out after a while.

And there were your live performances. Why didn't you take charge then? Why did you let them do that to you?"

That got Tom angry, something Robin had not seen.

"Listen, remember before we parted that summer you said that you did not belong to the LA world? Well I didn't either. I still don't. And it's not just me. The entertainment business belongs to the executives not the artists. We just make money for them. If we're lucky we get a decent cut, but even that is not always the case."

He was on a roll: "And they don't just create a sound for you. They create an image for you: peg and groom you a certain way, put a spin on who you are, throw you in with certain crowds, and it's shocking how quickly you get used to certain trappings and can't live without them. Before you know it you're not even yourself. And that's not even the worst of it. What's really cynical is that they create an image for you and then they sell it back to yourself. They know that you don't just buy the image, you get hooked on it. That's how bad it is."

"John Hartford didn't get hooked."

Tom looked at her, genuinely puzzled. "John? You know him?"

"I know he wrote your first hit. He's a great song writer—and a thinking man."

Tom broke into a wide grin. "So instead of looking up Russian writers I should have talked to John?"

Robin ignored the comment. He went on: "John is an exception. P. T. Barnum once said no one ever went broke underestimating the intelligence of the American public."

"I thought it was Mencken who said that."

"Who's Mencken? Anyway he could have said no

one ever went broke underestimating the public's standards of good taste."

"And it's all the fault of bad executives?"

"No it's not, I admit it. Artists become addicted to success. Can't live without those number one spots on the charts, the adoring fans, the parties... And you can't rest on your laurels either. You can fall from grace just as quickly as you randomly rose to its heights. You can't let that happen. Keeping yourself in the spotlight becomes an obsession. Besides, you've got to make as much money as you can because it could all dry up tomorrow. So you don't turn down anything. You say yes to this and yes to that. No one can keep up with that kind of frenzy naturally so you get all the unnatural help you can get. Booze, amphetamines, cocaine, pot, pretty girls throwing themselves at you... Gotta get through it all somehow, those endless tours, the interminable jetsetting, the cramped boredom of buses and hotel rooms, the noise, the glare of lights, the mobs..."

That was the longest outburst Robin had heard from Tom but he was not yet finished. "It's all a spiral of addiction. I don't care to moralize but I know this: addition takes away your freedom once and for all. You live forever in its shadow. And I live the nightmare of having set a precedent for my kids. I almost hope my ex poisons my kids against me so they want nothing to do with the life I have lived, even if that means not wanting to have to do anything with me."

They were silent. "I'm sorry to see you so despondent," she said.

"You don't know the half of it."

Robin felt bad. She wanted to make him feel better by letting him know how extraordinary she thought his singing was. She stumbled to put into words how she thought he landed his first notes like a swan gliding a touchdown on the surface of water. How he lent brightness to his voice the way he sang just a hair ahead of the beat. How he even sang his consonants...

"Sing my consonants?" he was amused.

"Most singers only hold notes on their vowels but you sing the consonants too, the voiced ones. Like Nat King Cole did." Then she fell silent, a little embarrassed that he might think it was presumptuous of her to talk shop to a pro.

"It's gratifying for a musician when people listen so closely," he sensed that she had cut her herself off. "What else do you like?"

"I love the way Louis Armstrong sings even the unvoiced vowels. I think he's the most brilliant stylist, his taste is impeccable. But you know who is my single most favorite? Janis—Janis Joplin. She even sings her breaths."

Tom was looking at her with amused fondness: "You're good audience."

"In fact," Robin went on, "your name should have been Bobby McGee."

Tom gave her a surprised look. He looked at her more intently, smiled, and shook his head. Then he stopped smiling and shook his head again.

She changed the subject: "I once heard you say that you thought Ray Charles was the greatest piano player and singer."

"I said that on a TV show," he sounded relieved. "So you did follow me a bit!"

"I heard things. For instance I heard it said that Tom Camden can harmonize with a backfiring truck," she laughed. "I didn't need to follow you, I kept stumbling upon you. Anyway I sensed how talented you were the first day we met. I understood there were heights to which you aspired." Then she hesitated a moment. "I also knew that because of your talent we had no future together."

He gave her a sad smile: "You were more aware of things back then than me."

"Virtuosity has a life of its own," she said.

Tom gave her another look in the soft earnest eyes of his youth.

Decades go by in the blink of an eye when you look back, but when you're inside time it goes through the hourglass one grain of sand at a time. Twenty-four hours is a long time. Tom still sang like an angel, played like the devil, and Robin loved listening to him. His voice was burnished and still strong but had lost the youthful glint that, in retrospect, did at times edge toward shrillness. His music had turned a little inward now. He no longer projected his sound like he was out to conquer all space around him, the world. He was long past proving anything to anybody. Leaning back on the sofa, putting his feet up and resting the guitar on his chest, sometimes just humming, he appeared to dissolve in music. Robin loved the private concerts.

"What are your plans now?" she asked as his stay drew to a close.

"I've got to get as many bookings as I can. I need to recover financially."

"Playing the same arrangements?"

"It's what the audience expects of me," he said, a little flustered: "I'm still nothing but a glorified session musician, except it pays better now. It's just a job, a business decision."

"I wonder…," Robin reflected. "I sometimes think the most important decisions in life are aesthetic ones. A line from one of my favorite poets says, only the voice remains. In your case, literally."

Tom didn't say anything. "What are your plans?" he asked.

"I'll tell you what…" she sat up. "I feel fulfilled. And now I want to live my fulfilled self. It might be absurd to say this at my age but I feel a spring wind stirring up new life in me. I feel rain has quenched the thirst of the ground under my feet. The earth feels pregnant again. Abundance is ahead. And this is what I am going to do: I am going to go my room, close the door behind me, and teach myself how to write by copying the masters. I'm a little behind you in that!"

───────────────

The day Tom left the sky was clear for the most part. When the cab came to pick him up he threw his suitcase in the trunk and slid his guitar in the backseat. A last embrace and the cab took off. He looked over his shoulder and waved at Robin through the back window. She stood by her door holding her dog in her arms. Once the cab blended into the traffic and she lost sight of him, she stepped inside, set her little dog down, and closed the door behind herself.

Published by **URTEXT*media***

www.urtext.us

URTEXT

Returning to Iran, Sima Nahan

The Blue Flower of Forgetfulness, Cyrus Samii

Zendegiye Koodakan, Jabbar and Samineh Baghcheban

Buna Nameh, Buna Alkhas

Red Finch

Over the Candlestick, Clara Middleton

Dear Oprah, Alireza Ansari

Mr. Clavi Chord, Trilby James and Rachel Long